The Benefits & Blessings of Fasting

Heavenly Strategies for Earthly Manifestation.

Jasmin Dareus

Copyright 2014 by Jasmin Dareus. Tree Of Life Publications. All Rights Reserved.

All scriptures quotations are from the King James Version of the Holy Bible.

No part of this book may be reproduced or transmitted in any form or by any means, electronic or mechanical, including photocopying and recording or by any information storage and retrieval system without permission from the author and publisher.

Title: The Benefits & Blessings of Fasting
      Heavenly Strategies for Earthly Manifestations

ISBN 9781503289451

Published By:

Tree Of Life Publications
P. O. Box F-44252
Freeport,
Grand Bahama,
Bahamas.

Printed in the United States of America

Table Of Contents

Dedication	4
Acknowledgement	5
Introduction	7
Chapter 1: Types of Fasting ………………………………..	11
Chapter 2 : How to Begin a Fast …………………………..	14
Chapter 3: Fasting & Prayer …………………………….…	19
Chapter 4: Fasting & The Word …………………………..	32
Chapter 5: Fasting As Spiritual Warfare ……………………..	35
Chapter 6: Fasting & The Prophetic ………………………..	40
Chapter 7: Benefits & Blessings of Fasting …………………	44
Chapter 8: Fasting & The Day Of Atonement …………….…	47
Chapter 9: Daily Prophetic Declarations …………………….	50
Chapter 10: 10 Keys of Kingdom Alignment ………………..	51
Chapter 11: Life After Fasting ……………………………..	53
Conclusion	56
Appendix- 8 Prayers	58
Bibliography	87

Dedication

The first of everything belongs to the Lord. Father, it is with honor that I present the book that burst my writing matrix to you. May you take pleasure in my first fruit offering.

ALL Blessing, and Honour and Glory and Power be unto Him that sitteth upon the throne and unto the Lamb forever and ever. Amen Rev. 5:13 (KJV)

Acknowledgement

I would like to acknowledge the Anglican Priests that had foundational development in my knowledge of Christ Jesus: Father John Kabiga, who taught me Greek and Hebrew in High School and wet my appetite for a deeper hunger of the word of God. Father Don Haynes, who further mentored me, discipled me in prayer and allowed me to deliver my first sermon. Father Haynes first recognized and steered me toward the holy call to priesthood on my life.

I would like to recognize Prophet Kirkwood Murphy who activated me in the Prophetic Realm, and his wife, first lady Kelly Murphy of Temple Fellowship Ministries, Nassau, Bahamas. Also, Prophetess Cyprianna Rolle, who helped me immensely in recognizing and walking in purity in the Prophetic and Apostle Rolle of New Birth Ministries, Nassau, Bahamas. I thank God for Dr. Allen Albury who helped to refine my leadership and intercession gifts.

Much thanks to Rev. Conrad Jones and Min. Lonna Jones of Church of God Peach Street for recognizing and supporting my writing ability.

Special Acknowledgement to Kingdom Harvest Global Ministries Freeport, Grand Bahama leadership team and members. Who allow me to lead them in prayer and intercession and construct prayers of deliverance for them . My team of spiritual Navy Seals and Snippers in the realm of the Spirit.

Heart Felt thanks to my covenant partners that sow in time, talent and treasure into Jasmin Dareus ministry weekly/monthly. Words do not adequately express my gratitude for your financial stability in advancing the Kingdom of God in your region. May the Lord reward you with a bountiful harvest. Tramayne Carroll, Bloneva Purcell, Catherine Smith, Patrice Smith-Russell, Marion Thompson and Curlene Campbell. Our off Island Members, Tiffany Wood, Renae Nesbitt and Anastacia Hoover. Especially, Deaconess Maggie Ferguson for supporting and believing in me, pushing me, and being a grandmother to my girls. I am forever grateful.

Sincere appreciation to my parents who brought me up in the fear and admonition of the Lord: Mr. Chilean Turner, Jr. of Cat Island and Mrs. Loretta Farrington & Leonard Farrington of Fresh Creek, Andros, Bahamas.

I am thankful for the leading ladies and jewels in my life that will learn this model of Fasting and Prayer first hand: my daughters B. Royalty, B. Majesty, B. Splendor Dareus.

Special mention of Mr. Ian & Barbara Rolle, Dr. Micheal & Susie Darville, Mrs. Dorothea Rolle, & Apostle Les & Shiela Bowling, Apostle Carlos & Prophetess Tiffany Reid of the Hope Center, Nassau who all contributed in some form or fashion to my life and ministry specifically during the production of this book and one of the most challenging periods of my life. Thank You!

Last but not least, much appreciation to my husband and Pastor, Apostle Brian Dareus for pushing me in the things of the Kingdom of God, allowing me opportunities to preach and for provoking me to new dimensions in fasting and prayer.

Introduction

The Spirit of the Lord is preparing spiritual stallions to be used in His end time army. I truly believe the readying of this remnant regime is coming to a rise to lead the battle against the Goliaths, Pharoahs, and Principalic spirits of this age. Our manes and coats are being carefully and surreptitiously stroked by the very hand of God whilst our spiritual muscles gain strength and our velocity, acceleration, in tandem and momentum with Him that called us out of darkness to shine in His marvelous light.

Today marks the beginning of the best days of your life! You will literally wonder after you have begun this journey why you hadn't started fasting and seeking the Lord with this kind of intensity and propensity earlier. Buckle up, get ready because you are in for an explosive experience in your spiritual life and soulical nature that will be forced to manifest in your natural realm. The Bible declares that the "Kingdom of heaven suffereth violence and the violent take it back by force" (Matt. 11:12 KJV). That's right, you are taking back some things with applied pressure in the realm of the spirit that rightfully belong to you.

I was introduced to fasting as an activity early in my Christian walk at the very onset of my conversion. Honestly, I felt the Holy Spirit leading me to do 4 specific things my first year of moving into the Kingdom: reading the word daily, spend time in prayer, fast regularly and gather with other believers at church, all of which are foundational and help to stabilize, strengthen and sustain you especially during turbulent times.

The word fasting occurs 17 times in the Bible and the word fast occurs 85 times in scripture. Fasting is a means of legal entry into the causal realm or spiritual realm. The term Fasting is derived from the Hebrew word: **tsom** which refers to the practice of self denial. It also comes from the Greek word: **nesteia** which means to deny oneself. Fasting then, is the abstaining and denial from physical food for spiritual purposes and natural results. It is the humbling and afflicting of one's soul before the Creator. Fasting, though spiritual, undoubtedly brings divine alignment and promotes order in every area of our lives. One of the ultimate ways of drawing closer to God is through this observance. The book Of James in chapter

4 verse 8 (KJV) states that "if we draw night to God, He will draw nigh unto us". During this time of consecration, our food is literally the word of God. In the beginning was the word and the word was with God and the word was God (John 1:1 KJV). You will have great delight feasting upon Him and dwelling in Him and in His Presence. In His Presence is fullness of joy and at His right hand there are pleasures forevermore (Psalm 6:11 KJV-Emphasis mine). Understand that Fasting is the will of God for the believer's life and is a spiritual principle that must be upheld.

*Matthew 6: 16 "**Moreover when ye fast**, be not as the hypocrites, of a sad countenance: for they disfigure their faces, that they may appear unto men to fast. Verily I say unto you, They have their reward". (KJV)*

As disciples we fast for many reasons, at specific seasons and before making major decisions in our lives. We fast for:

1. **Direction from the Lord** when it seems as if you've arrived at a dead end or cross road and need to know His divine will and plan for your life; "For the Lord knoweth the way of the righteous" (Psalm 1:6 KJV). Ezra 8:21 Psalm 16:11 /Psalm 27:11 /Psalm 119:35/ Psalm 119:35 / Isaiah 43:16/Joel 2:8

2. **We fast to loose the bands of wickedness and let the oppressed go free and to destroy every yoke** (Isaiah 58:6 KJV). In ministry when facing a deliverance case or destroying yokes of bondage that is rather stubborn, you and or your deliverance team fast to break the yoke and let the demonically oppressed go free. Generational bondages and curses over our own lives and the lives of our children. Each case is different and some may require more time than others. Some may be a 3 day fast or 7 days depending on the leading of the Holy Spirit.

3. **Ordination into ministry or service of the Lord.**
"Separate unto me Barnabas and Saul for the work whereunto I have called them" (Acts 13:2 KJV). It is critically important before entering the work and service of the Lord to have a spent a season in some time in Fasting. Particularly important as well is the need to fast for spiritual leadership especially if they are going off track from assignment and also if you need to see a fresh move of the Holy Spirit in your local assembly.

4. **National Crises or facing the judgment of God.** Esther fasted for 3 days for the Jewish People and as a result was successful in having an annihilation judgment concerning her people over turned. We also see judgment being negated in the book of Jonah chapter 3 (KJV) when the king proclaimed a fast for the entire nation (which included man, woman, children and animals) and the Lord lifted the sentence from over Ninevah. Please note, this is a very serious fast, as all are but in this one, no food or water is to be drunken for the duration of the time. Be spirit led and confirm with your spiritual leaders and or Pastor (s).

5. **Spiritual Warfare.** There are specific times and or seasons in our lives when the attacks oncoming are tremendous. Not one right after the other, but you get like three hits all at once. It's almost like a Job experience, the moment you hear bad news, another is a second away. Help and hope is here. Fasting aids in us developing mastery in the usage of our spiritual weaponry. It may also unveil a new level of artillery for the new plane on or about to be entered. The Holy Ghost will "gird you with strength for battle", "teach your hands to war and your fingers to fight" enabling you to break the fiery arrows of the enemy and He will "make your feet like hinds' feet" for you to run through the enemy troops and leap over the enemy walls of obstruction (Psalm 18:29-36- Emphasis mine).

6. **For Healing & Deliverance**
The writer of the book of Isaiah says when we fast our "health shall spring forth speedily" (Isa. 58:8 KJV)

"But He was wounded for our transgressions, He was bruised for our iniquities. The chastisement of our peace was upon Him and with His stripes we are healed" (Isa 53:5)

Deut 7:15 *"And the LORD will take away from thee all sickness, and will put none of the evil diseases of Egypt, which thou knowest, upon thee; but will lay them upon all them that hate thee"*

Ps 107:19-20 *"Then they cry unto the LORD in their trouble, and he saveth them out of their distresses. He sent his word, and healed them, and delivered them from their destructions".*

Jer 30:17" *For I will restore health unto thee, and I will heal thee of thy wounds, saith the LORD;...."*

7. **To have intimacy and fellowship with the Lord.** Sometimes even if it is for one day, it is good just to go before the Lord and not ask for anything, give Him no complaints but just to sit in His presence and hear what's on the Father's heart. He longs for us to know His heartbeat. (John 15:4-11 KJV) You will undoubtedly be refreshed, rejuvenated and rewarded for spending quality time with the king (Psalm 16:11)

Types of Fast

There are four (4) types of fasts listed in the Bible. At certain times the Lord will instruct you as to how long to fast and there are other times when He will direct you what not to eat on your fast. Of course, there will also be periods when you know you need to fast and the one chosen will be of your own volition. Caution, never attempt fasting to lose weight or for physical detoxification or beautification purposes. These are nonetheless direct by products but must never be main goal.

"And Jesus being full of the Holy Ghost returned from Jordan, and was led up into the widerness being forty (40) days tempted of the devil. (Luke 4:1 KJV)"

Fasting, then is also a means of spiritual elevation. It is a time of specialized ops training and sharpening of gifts/skills and intensifying and purifying of your anointing.

Types of Fasting:

- ❖ **40 Day Fast**
    The 40 day fast is known as a ministry fast. This type of fast should only be done under the auspices of the Holy Ghost of God. This is not a common fast. Usually done by ministry gifts (Apostles, Prophets, Teachers, Evangelists, Pastors), especially prophets. You may fast during this time with fruits and vegetables and all natural juice. You can also fast from sunrise to sunset with no food. There is the option of having just one meal a day in the evening. I have done this fast a few times and it literally shifted my life and ministry into the right and a higher gear. This type of fast causes you to walk in the anointings read about in the Holy Bible. This fast enables one to walk in effective ministry and impact their generation for the glory of God. This type of fast was completed in scripture by Moses, Elijah, Ezekiel and Jesus. (Luke 4, 1 Kings 14:8, Eze 4:6, Deut. 10:10 KJV).

    * Not exclusive to ministry gifts. Consult your Pastor/Leader before attempting this type of fast for guidance. Not recommended for babes in Christ.

- ❖ **Esther Fast or Absolute Fast**
  Queen Esther and all the Jews fasted for three (3) days without food and without water. Crises times demand critical moves in the realm of the spirit. The king of Ninevah did the same fast and had the nation fast along with him. This method of fasting should only be completed through instruction by the Holy Spirit and in times of national crises. (Esther 4:16, Jonah 3:7). Consult your Pastor/Leader before attempting this fast especially if you are a babe in Christ.

- ❖ **Daniel Fast**
  Also known as the partial fast. Daniel fasted in periods of time for 10 days, 14 days, and 21 days with fruits and vegetables. The scripture says he ate "no pleasant bread, neither came flesh or meat in my mouth" (Dan 10:3 KJV). I have found this to be one of the easiest fast to accomplish especially if you love food. I have done these types countless of times and it is not difficult. If you look at the length of time, you may get discouraged but you can do it! You can do all things through Christ who strengthens you (Phil 4:13).

- ❖ **John the Baptist**
  The prophet John ate wild locust and honey which consisted of his daily intake. Some call it a fast but sometimes you would find prophets especially having their food intake specified by the Lord as seen with Elijah, and Isaiah. Particularly in the cases of John the Baptist and Daniel, this was not just a fast but a designated way of life before the Lord.

This type of fast is not listed in scripture but I know it works:

Rotational Fast/Chain Fast- For those with severe health issues, particularly can attempt this method. As a church body you can fast for 12 days if you have 12 committed members to each consecrate one day. A prayer group can also utilize this one. This can get everyone involved.

Fasting should be a regular practice in the life of believers. I can accredit many advancements, promotions and acceleration in my life due to constant fasting and prayer. My personal ministry began in 2007 and in 2009 at the age of twenty seven (27) my husband and I were instructed by the Holy Spirit and from a counsel of elders to establish a ministry. I am certain it was my destiny but being faithful to fasting helped to clear the path for movement both physically and spiritually in my life.

It is not the length of the fast that is important; it is the heart and spirit of the individual fasting. Fasting longer does not make one more spiritual especially with the wrong motive and spirit. Sometimes, one may have to fast longer due to the amount of things they need to loose over themselves or bondages that need to be broken. A short fast could mean you just have a few things to work out. Pay more attention to the state of your spirit during this time. If needed, you will be prompted to increase fasting activity by Holy Spirit or Spiritual leader.

How To Begin A Fast

My first time fasting I made it to day 2 and ate because of the headache. After that, I was determined to make it through the second time around and I did it. If you are a novice to fasting I would encourage you to start skipping a meal a day or two before your actual fast begins; thereby acclimatizing your body to the process. Even if you have tried before and failed, that is ok. You are not the first and you will not be the last. Just mean business with God and commit your time, mind, energy, body, spirit and soul to Him. He is able to keep that which we commit unto Him.

This is not a hard and fast rule but it will help you tremendously. Follow closely.

The veil was torn in the temple and now we have been granted free access to the Father. Hallelujah!!!!! Glory be to God! If you are a new convert, 7 days is very ambitious so I recommend three for starters. You can proceed with 7 after or if led to by the Spirit of the Lord. Just take the first 3 days of Scriptural reading.

Fasting Format. Have a Fasting Diary to journal in.

Title: Fasting Forward

7 Days of Fasting (Consecration): List Dates
Starting Time:
End Time:

Fasting Purpose: Detail (Write Down: Write the Vision)

- A. Family Members (Spouse/children/cousins/etc)
- B. Your local ministry or church
- C. Signs, Wonders, Miracles, Breakthrough
- D. To Destroy Ungodly Habits/Cycles
- E. Healing for yourself or loved one
- F. Increase Faith
- G. Ministry Leaders/Political Leaders/National Issues
- H. Your Island, City, State and or Nation
- I. A Refreshing In your Spirit

* See Chapter on Benefits & Blessings of Fasting to List More.

Fasting Forward Guidelines:

>   1. Fasting is never done for show! Only those that need to know you are fasting are to be told: husband, wife, Pastor. This is a very critical time in a believer's walk and you should not be broadcasting that you are fasting. (Matt. 6:16-18)
>
>   2. If you are fasting from sunrise to sunset each day. Fruits and vegetables may be eaten. Drink only 100% juice and plenty of water as this will serve as a time of detoxification and purification as well; both to your body and soul even though it is a spiritual event.
>
>   3. Abstain from Television, magazines, gossip, gossip columns and people, negative and or idle talk, obscene language and bad company. Sample reading outline is listed below. (Romans 6:13)
>
>   4. Restrict your movements or daily activity to necessities: going to school, work, grocery shop, or church. This is to minimize infiltration or contamination from demonic sources to sap your strength. If you can get alone for a 3 day fast that will be great but failing that, the restrictions are a must to gain maximum impact.
>
>   5. Caution!!!!! You may start to feel nauseous, dizzy, light headed, get headache, start shaking but be not alarmed. These are only withdrawal symptoms which occur the 1st or 2nd day. By day 3 you will be rolling. You may also start having some serious symptoms of depression or anxiety. Have no fear and don't you stop. It is a plan of the enemy that lets you know you are on track so stay on point. Once this has occurred, you have automatically gained territory.
>
>   6. Guard against spiritual attacks. The real fight will not be going without food. Trust me, the Devil will loose more dark forces against you in persons close to you, areas least expected or through strangers. This sign will be symbolic of the new level of anointing

you are walking in and the power and authority God has given to you (Luke 10:19).

7. Increase your daily prayer time. If you normally pray for a total 30 minutes per day. Increase that to one hour per day. You can do 30 minutes in the morning and 30 minutes at night. Or if your total time is 20 min per day, then double that. Intense prayer will enable you to continue this journey without fainting. Amplify reading the word as well because this will be your only nourishment until fast is completed. As you humble your soul and draw near to God, He will also draw near to you (James 4: 8). His presence will be undeniable and unmistakable. Daniel 9:3

8. Please rest during this time (Mark 6:31). Spend time alone with the Holy Ghost as He will be speaking and revealing Himself to you. (Mark 4:34). Sometimes just getting away in solitude so the Lord can have us for Himself and to Himself.

9. Be ready to see your own physical problems surface. Point fingers at no one. This is also your time to self evaluate. Be open because you never know just what the Lord might say.

10. Keep a journal and write down all dreams, scriptures, cliches', poems, songs (secular or spiritual) that you have during this time. Make special notation as to places, time/date, how you feel, colours, metals, symbols and numbers. Be elaborate in description. You will develop your own pattern of hearing and or seing in the realm of the spirit and your unique dream language. Keep your pad with you at all times because the Holy Spirit will use the most unusual things at the most unexpected places and people to minister to you at this time. Be alert, be still, don't discriminate, and listen for the still small voice. Father has used secular and unconventional songs to minister to me. Be open. He will make you laugh and smile.

11. Fasting is no substitute for your regular work and or study. For example, if you are a student or you have a business meeting during this time. Do put in your quality time with the Lord but also spend

time to prepare for your event. He will however, give you favour as a shield (Psalm 5), download supernatural information to you, and make His face to shine upon you.

12. Absolutely no sex during this time. Husbands and wives are to gain permission from one another before fasting.

Reading Schedule: Everyday you open your eyes, arise with enormous anticipation that God will feed you with fresh manna from His Word. Can you taste it now? Smile. Uhhhmmm. The smell of Rhema word.

*Suggestion- Read half material in morning and the other half at night or equal portion so you can read a piece at noon day. If you are real hungry and read all material before hand, continue with the scriptures given or allow the Holy Ghost to guide you to more scriptures.

Day 1
Morning Isaiah 58 *Flag Scripture*
Proverb 1, 2
Joel 1, 2, 3

Day 2
Morning Isaiah 58
Proverbs 3, 4, 5
Esther 1-4

Day 3
Morning Isaiah 58
Proverbs 6, 7, 8
Esther 5-9

Day 4
Morning Isaiah 58
Proverbs 9, 10, 11, 12
Matthew 5-10

Day 5
Morning Isaiah 58
Proverbs 13, 14, 15, 16
2 Chronicles 1 – 8

Day 6
Morning Isaiah 58
Proverbs 17, 18, 19, 20
Acts 1 – 9

Day 7
Morning Isaiah 58
Proverbs 21, 22, 23, 24
Nehemiah 1 -13

On your Mark..

                    Get Ready..

                                      Let's Go…

Fasting & Prayer

Prayer travels at the speed of the spirit and knows no racial, cultural, gender, geographical, educational or political boundary. Prayer recalibrates atmospheres, shifts environments, alters climates, governs nations and legislates in the realm of the spirit. Prayer and fasting is a dynamite duo; together, they are a destructive force against the kingdom of darkness.

I believe that prayer is one of the secret weapons of the church. Prayer is powerful beyond human reasoning. The Holy Spirit said to me one day, the reason the enemy fights prayer so vigorously is because true prayer releases a spirit of unity and unity is strength and power. Genesis chapter 11 and verse 6 states" And the Lord said, Behold the people is one, and they have all one language; and this they begin to do: and now nothing will be restrained from them, which they have imagined to do."

A people that will yield themselves to prayer can achieve anything because unity will be a bond. A people that will fast and pray would be explosive in their field and their very presence would wreak havoc on Satan's kingdom.

"Every art unfolds its secrets and its beauty only to the man who practices it! The humble soul that is always bowed in prayer, to him will the secrets of the Lord be revealed. " Andrew Murray

"Men are always to pray and not faint". Luke 18:1. Who God is gives weight to what He asks.

What Is Prayer?
- ❖ Prayer is simple communication between man and his deity.
- ❖ It is the discipline and habit of every day running into the presence of God before we get before others. Our prayer life denotes our relationship with the Lord.
- ❖ Prayer is commitment and covenant.
- ❖ Prayer is a crucifixion of our flesh

- ❖ Prayer is our opportunity to be real with God. James 4:2 "Ye have not because ye ask not"
- ❖ Prayer expresses our confidence in God.

"Beloved, if our heart condemn us not, then we have confidence toward God. And whatsoever we ask, we receive of Him, because we keep His commandments, and do those things that are pleasing in His sight

- ❖ Prayer invokes the perfect will of God in the now.
- ❖ Prayer is to be done with conviction. It is to be undertaken with passion and fervency. This type of prayer is irresistible, indispensable and availeth much.
- ❖ Make no mistake about it, the art of praying is a spirit.

It is possible to be praying, in deep dimensions of prayer, a prayer warrior but still neglect the daily devoted time before the Lord. One must have a rock solid revelation of who God is to be endowed with power in prayer and have usage of the keys of the kingdom.

- ❖ Prayer is not a duty it is a commandment. Luke 18:1.

Prayer is not to be done as a duty, it is for our spirit, soul and body to be given to; every part of our being. We think we lose time, money and friends, needless to say opportunities when we spend time in prayer. However, the man who gives all in prayer, or loses all to prayer will undoubtedly find ALL in prayer.

- ❖ Jericho walls, double chains, iron gates, mountains, boulders and soldiers all must give way to prayer.

What things soever ye desire when ye pray, believe that ye received them, and ye shall have them." Mark 11:24

A component or element of true, prevailing prayer is the element of desire. Desire is to yearn for the possession of; to entreat and to long for. One of The causes of insufficient or unsuccessful prayer is the lack of desire. Desire is a secret power that moves the world.

- ❖ Prayer, I believe, is the breath of the almighty, the force of His kingdom and the power to prevail in impossible situations. Prayer and Fasting is the secret to a believer's success. Hence, prayer and fasting will make you unstoppable, unblockable, indestructible, undeniable and unkillable.

"Ye shall seek me, and shall find me, when ye shall search for me with all your heart." Jeremiah 29:13

Prayer is where everything begins and ends in the realm of the Spirit. Prayer is the genuine genetic code of the church. I believe the destiny of humanity is changed and charted through the power of potent prayer.

Types of prayer

Intercession
The Greek word for Intercession is" pagah" which means to impinge (to invade or interrupt) by accident or by violence. Further defined asto encroach or to advance beyond the usual limit. Also, it means to fall upon. The boundary you are to reach in life will never be reached if not interceded into. Intercession involves forcefully taking territory, and conquering . Intercession is warfare, battle, wrestling and interrupting the powers of darkness.

In intercession, the person praying shares in the burden that Christ Jesus feels for a person, place or circumstance anywhere in the world. We then, in intercession, partake of Christ's suffering. We enter into our priestly function of providing an earthly base for God's heavenly mandates. Intercession literally makes the natural subject to the realm of the Kingdom of God. Thy kingdom Come, thy will be done, on earth as it is in heaven.

I believe that the prayer of intercession breathes life and manifests miracles for those interceding for (Elisha in 2 Kings 4:29-34). The Holy Spirit said to me one night as I interceded, heavily burdened and deeply broken in Spirit, you don't have to knock when you come to me my child. I expect to meet you at certain times and you very rarely disappoint me. So the door is always left open for you. If you find for some reason the door is locked, use your keys. For I have given you keys to the kingdom. Intercessors possess the Keys to the Kingdom of Heaven.
"And I will give unto thee the keys of the Kingdom of heaven: and whatsoever thou shalt bind on earth shall be bound in heaven: and whatsoever thou shalt loose on earth shall be loosed in heaven." Matthew 16:19

Intercessors stand in the gap for people, and nations that cannot or refuse to do it themselves. Intercessors are like arrows, bright as lightning bolts, ready for the Lord's command. We intercept, interject and interrupt satan's plans and schemes spiritually for a natural manifestation (Col 2:15) of heaven's declaration over our lives.

Jeremiah 27:18 "But if they be prophets, and if the word of the Lord be with them, let them now make intercession to the Lord of hosts that the vessels which be left in the house of the Lord, and in the house of the King of Judah go not to Babylon." Intercession keeps God's people out of captivity and bondage. It also strengthens those in place of authority to carry out the will of God in the earth.

Intercession is the type of prayer needed to penetrate nations closed to hearing the gospel (Acts 14:27/2 Cor 2:12). China and Russia along with all the other non Christian nations were penetrated and broken through in intercession first in the realm of the spirit. Oh believer, the Lord is still looking for a man/woman to make up the hedges. Will you intercede at His beckoning? The very fact that you are reading this signifies your call to the ministry of intercession.

Intercession releases the mind of the Spirit and the perfect will of God for the believer's life (Luke 6:12-16/John 5:19). Intercession should be done before all major decisions in your life. Before Jesus chose His 12 disciples, He interceded all night which presents us with a biblical pattern that we should follow. Intercession is so important it is single reason Jesus lives and is seated at the right hand of our Father (Hebrews 7:25). He ever liveth to make intercession for us.

Characteristics Of Intercessors

Intercessors must be devoted. Ministers, especially full time ministers should all intercede.

Intercessors must be patient. The Bible says that Simeon waited on the consolation of Israel. Daniel interceded for the fury and anger of the Lord to be taken away and for God's chosen people to be released from captivity. (Dan 9)

Intercessors must be filled with the Holy Ghost. Only the Holy Spirit can help you carry the weight of intercession.

God must be able to trust you. You must be found faithful.

Intercessors are men/women who are dreamers and have visions.

Intercessors must be selfless. Father may require hours when you want to run errands, go to hair salon or even travel or better yet, sleep. You will just have to back yourself, your flesh on the side and let the Lord have His Holy Way. That is easier said than done. However, in the interest of our King and for the commonwealth of His Kingdom it is but a slight task. One that we are privileged as intercessors to carry out. The Lord spoke to me about intercessors and said true intercessors always show up before His throne at a specific time. They are faithful to meet their prayer times and always find the door open and Father waiting to greet them. The Holy Spirit said, it is like a parent that expects a child home every evening at a specific hour, the door will be left open for him so there is no need to knock. However, faithful intercessors will also pick up emergency calls from the spirit if a watchman has left or abandoned post (specific hour/additional prayer time).

Prayer Of Supplication

The prayer of supplication is a prayer of petition before the throne of the Lord. Phillipians 4:6 says "Be careful for nothing, but in everything by prayer and supplication with thanksgiving make your requests be made known unto God. " Consider, in the book of Revelations chapter 5 and verse 8 which speaks of "Prayer Vials" that are filled with the prayers of the saints. I believe that these vials or bowls must be filled with our prayers before they are actually poured out in manifestation on our behalf. Acts chapter 3(verses 1-10) talks about Peter and John going to the temple at the hour of prayer. A man lame from his mother's womb was their asking alms of those that passed. Peter said to him, "Silver and Gold have I *none; but such as I have I give unto thee: In the name of Jesus Christ of Nazereth rise up and walk.*" Peter then lifted up this man to his feet and his ankle bones received strength. After meditating and studying this type of prayer the Holy Ghost brought this scripture to me. He said the prayer vials of Peter and John were full because praying in the temple was a habit that they kept daily. Obviously they saw Jesus keep a prayer pattern and practiced it to reap the same results.

My husband and I were pastoring and living in the church. Having to bathe before members came in and eat after they left. Additionally, my car had gone to the grave on me; so we were also walking. After one year of intense daily prayer, a house was released to us and a car sown into our lives. I believe our prayer vials began to run over. One of the reasons there are few to no miracles in churches is because the prayer vials above that local house/assembly is empty. Hence, the importance of an active prayer ministry or intercessory team. We've got to reinstitute the foundation of prayer, that of supplication and petition in the local churches. Pastor, Apostle, Prophet, prayer leaders please get those that are at ease and asleep in Zion to now awake and arise to prayer.

Please note dear reader, this type of prayer is so we ask Father for what we need. The time to petition the King. Isaiah chapter 1 talks about going to the Father to reason with Him. The Bible says to ask and it shall be given to you; and whatsoever you ask in my name shall be done. However, what do you do when Father prolongs the answer or says NO? You just keep praying knowing that God is never late and always on time. Furthermore, when God says NO, it is for our benefit and the blessing of the body. Father does not owe us an explanation. Let's reference Jesus praying the prayer of supplication in the garden of Gethsemane. The Bible says Jesus prayed "…if it be possible, let this cup pass from me…" 3 times (Matthew 26:39-46) and because He truly desired the perfect will of God, in spite of the suffering, in spite of the shame and pain, he was about to encounter, God's answer was NO. Jesus prayed for the same thing thrice. Whoever told you to pray once for a matter and leave it because praying again demonstrates a lack of faith has not fully read scripture? Jesus, our model, showed us exactly the pattern for the prayer of petition and supplication.

"If a son shall ask bread of any of you that is a father, will he give him a stone? Or if he asks a fish, will he for a fish give him a serpent?" Luke 11:11.

Personally, if it were possible, I believe that I would do my best to weary the Lord in supplication. I mean that! A better understanding and example comes from the unjust judge in the book of Luke 18. Luke 18:5 "Yet because this widow troubleth me, I will avenge her, lest by her continual coming she weary me."

Luke 18:7-8 "And shall not God avenge his own elect which cry day and night unto him, though he bear long with them? I tell you that He will avenge them speedily……." The spirit of supplication and petition places you in line for a speedy move of the Lord.

Prayer Of Agreement/Corporate Prayer

Matthew 18:19-20 "Again I say if any two of you agree on the earth, concerning anything that they ask it will be done for them by my Father in heaven. For where two or three are gathered together in my name, I am there in the midst of them."

The prayer of agreement is a powerful kingdom key neglected in most Christian communities. Prayer meeting is the least attended meeting in the majority of churches. The average believer lacks the knowledge of this powerful prayer technique. There is an extremely explosive power that comes from agreement in prayer. The scripture says that *it will be done*, not that it may be possible but that it shall be done! Hallelujah! There is strength in numbers. One can put a thousand to flight; two can put 10,000 to flight; three can put 100,000 to flight and four puts 1,000,000 to flight. We thus see that praying alone is great but joining faith with another believer, it is 10,000 times better. There are times when you pray on your own for your family needs and day to day operations. That is fine. However, for the weightier matters, especially in the body of Christ, we should join shields and link faith in the prayer of agreement. When Peter was imprisoned, the church in the book of Acts all got together in the prayer of Agreement and that Prayer Task Force released an angel who immediately escorted Peter from Prison. When there is a terminal illness in the body and major attacks or critical national concerns, it's time to call in the experts and special task force; those that are anointed to pierce and penetrate the heavens. You know those among you that love to pray and have victory in their own personal prayer life.

Because the blessings of the Lord rests on unity (Psalm 133) and his presence when we agree in His name, the devil seeks to keep the body divided with jealousy, envy, bitterness, confusion and anger. Prayer must not be done to sound eloquent or super spiritual but rather come from a place of purity and humility that the Father may be glorified.

The prayer of Agreement commands God's blessings and God's blessings produces multiplication. True and genuine prayers of agreement are a mighty force in the realm of the Spirit. This type of prayer releases multiplied power and yields great results.

Acts 4:31 "After they prayed, the place where they were meeting was shaken. And they were all filled with the Holy Spirit and spoke the word of God boldly."
When a city or nation needs to be shaken, the prayer of agreement should be employed. Believers must learn to lock shields now to shake out the darkness that

prevail and cause the will of God to be loosed in the earth realm as a people but it will take a unified, corporate effort. The level of infilling of the Holy Ghost and spirit of boldness on believers are released as a result of this prayer of agreement. Their prayer was specific, fervent and effective.

This type of prayer also releases the captives from prison and break shackles (Acts 16:25).

Ecclesiastes says two have a better reward for their labour than one (chapter 4:4). Husband and wives, parent and children, pastors and members, fellow laborers in the body are perfect examples. Employ discernment and follow the leading of the Holy Spirit when selecting a partner because people may appear close to you but will not come in agreement with you for the manifestation you seek.

Miracles, Breakthroughs and Revivals are birthed and pulled down by the mighty prayer warriors in the church who focus, concentrate and target their prayers effectively and harmoniously.

Prayer is so powerful that the disciples asked Jesus to teach them how to pray. Jesus' life was so saturated with prayer that He had the Spirit of God without measure and was able to perform great miracles as a direct result. He didn't teach the disciples how to "Preach", "Prophesy" or operate in any other gift, he taught them the powerful and holy pattern of prayer. Lord teach us to pray and give us the grace to continue in prayer.

All Night Prayer Meeting

I remember the Lord speaking to me in a vision in the year 2006 about lying all night before Him. I went straight to the book of Joel because I knew that scripture was there.
"Gird yourselves, and lament, ye priests: howl, ye ministers of the alter: come, lie all night in sackcloth, ye ministers of my God: for the meat offering and drink offering is withholden from the house of your God. Sanctify ye a fast, call a solemn assembly, gather the elders and all inhabitants of the land into the house of the Lord your God and cry unto the Lord...." Joel 1:13,14

One night encounter with God can change your life and give you a 24 hour turn around. You will pay a sacrificial price in time, and energy but it will be worth it. This type of prayer are for desperate believers. Desperate times demand desperate measures. It is amazing how we all want dumbfounding miracles in our lives but we will not do anything different to obtain it. This is also the type of prayer that will loose a spirit of prayer over you if you truly desire it. The fire for prayer will be lit on your alter during this time. You will have to keep the flames burning yourself and stay disciplined.

Praying In Tongues
I recommend not just praying a specified time a day but spending time praying specifically in the Holy Ghost. Speaking in tongues frequently divinely connects us to the Spirit of God which knows the mind of God. When we speak in tongues, the bible says in the spirit we speak mysteries which is the Greek word "mysterion" meaning you retrieve information not givien to ordinary mortals, secrets are released not obvious to natural understanding, and you know the counsel which governs God in dealing with the righteous withheld from the wicked. We then grow rapidly in perception, understanding and relationship as to what God is doing and how we are to assist him. As spiritually beings, our spirits are more perceptive than our minds. Hence, the reason you just know things without physical foreknowledge. Our spirits see things before our minds so this is a major reason the enemy wouldn't want you speaking in tongues and carnal folk would make fun of you. Speaking in tongues is extremely powerful because you contact eternity, immediately. There is no value we can ever place on that.

Benefits of Speaking in tongues:
*Hidden Wisdom of God released into our spirit nmand downloaded to our soul.
   The wisdom of God is naturally veiled in a mystery according to scripture and
   Praying in tongues unveils this mystery to us.
*Revelation of the Deep & Secret things of God (1 Corin 2:10)
  (1 Corin 2:7)
*Knowledge of God & Man (2 Corin 2:11)
*Spiritual Comparative Techniques (2 Corin 2:13)
*Faith Builder (Jude 1:20)
*Edifies & Stregthens & Establishes the Believer in life and Destiny (1 Corin 14:4)
*Spiritual Discernment is sharpened and heightened (1Corin 2:14)
*Necessary for dreamers/dream interpreters
*Gives Prophetic Accuracy
*Helps Us Pray Effectively (Romans 8:26)
*Makes known the Perfect Will Of God
*Helps our infirmities (meaning sickness, weaknesses, trials and troubles)
*Gateway into the supernatural

The gift and practicing of speaking in tongues is not a guarantee for spiritual purity but if practiced, and understood will lead you there.

The following are prayer times that will help you to understand why the Lord has been waking you up the same hour every morning. For some Father has been knocking on your door, window, calling your name or even touching you around the same time each day. That is your "Prayer Watch". You will understand what to pray for also during those prayer times, see how important and effective they are.

Jewish day is from sunset to sunset in 8 equal parts. There are 8 prayer watches all in 3 hour intervals.

First Prayer Watch.
6 pm – 9 pm Time For New Beginning

- Time to cancel curses over family, church, nation and execute judgement on the wicked (Is17:12-14/Psalm 149)
- Time to renew covenant with the Lord
- Time to pray for the preservation of ministries, projects, assignments, fruits, gifting and callings

Second Prayer Watch
9 pm -12 midnight   Time of Exaltation, Worship & Warfare

- Time to be alert as witches start their nightly activity of casting spells and curses around midnight.
- Time for regaining the spoils and bounty stolen from the enemy. Time of favour and supernatural release (Ex 3:21/Acts 23:23
- Time for radical praise, warfare, worship and intense prayer. The spirit of grace and supplication is released (Zec 9:12)
- Time to Move Now and pray for divine protection (Psa 3:1-7/Acts 9:23)

Third Prayer Watch
12 midnight – 3 am Time For Divine Government

- Time for deep spiritual warfare as this is a critical time of heightened demonic activity
- Time to overturn and overrule demonic decrees and be proactive in the spiritual realm
- Time to utterly slay and destroy the enemy

- Time to pray for marriages or married partners (Matt 25:6/ Ruth 3:1-10). Pray for happy married strategies.
- Time to speak peace into storms and turbulent situations.
- Time of most dreams (Job 4:13-14)

Fourth Prayer Watch
3 am – 6 am Time Of Morning Commanders

- Final leg and one of the most crucial portions of the night. Most demonic "henchmen" are scurrying home from their activities so as not to get caught. This is the time to cancel, pull down, uproot, break, cut, nullify and dismantle every scheming plot, tactic, plan, programme, policies, judgments, entrapments, webs and assignment of the enemy against your life with the sword of the Lord (Heb 4:12/Psa 29). Shake the wicked totally out of your day (Job 38:12)
- Time to command your morning and make your dayspring to know its place (order your day) Job 38:12. Your morning has a womb so impregnate it with the seed you want to manifest throughout the day (Psalm 110:3). The morning has wings thus giving you the ability to take flight once you catch this watch.(Psa 139:9). This is also the time of visitation (Is 33:2/50:4)
- Even Jesus rose a great while before day (Mark 1:35) to pray the will of the Father.
- Time when the Lord releases angels to roll away stones of reproach, financial difficulty, business blockages, family feuds, obstacles to success and progress.

Fifth Prayer Watch
6am- 9am: Late Morning Watch

- Time to bold make apostolic and prophetic declarations Acts 2:15 Psalm 2:7-9.
- Decree as the sun rise, it will arise with "righteousness and healing in its wings" for your prayer life, family, relationships, city, nation, government and for the body of Christ.
- This is also the time for you to arise and shine (Is. 60:1) and a time of great outpouring of the Holy Spirit (Acts 1:8) along with being equipped by the Spirit of the Lord for your specific assignment.

Sixth Prayer Watch
9 am – 12 noon Exit & Entry Watch

- Time to pray for manifestation of prophetic promises, increase and fruitfulness. Time to rebuild. Ez. 36:26-30
- Time to pray and forgive those that offended and hurt us. Time to pull on the benefits of the cross: healing, power, forgiveness, access to the Father, prosperity. Mark 15:25
- Time to pray that you be conformed to the image of Christ Jesus and mortify the deeds of the flesh. (Rom 8:12-15).
- Pray that love will have her perfect work in your life
  Hebrews 13:21   James 1:43
- Pray that destruction that wasteth at noon day nor the fiery darts of the enemy will not be able to find you as you dwell in the secret place of the Most High and abide under the shadow of the Almighty God (Psalm 91)

Seventh Prayer Watch
12 noon – 3pm Hour Of Prayer

- Time when sun is at its highest so time to pray for the best which is the finished work of the cross to be fully actualized in your life: fruit of the spirit, gifts of the spirit, anointing, favour and glory of the Lord in every department of your life
- Time not to give in to temptation.
- Keep your eyes on the prize and stay focused.

Eight Prayer Watch
3 pm – 6 pm Transformation Watch

- This is the hour of grace and revelation and also the time to lift limitations (Luke 23:45-46)
- Time of establishment of God's kingdom in righteousness, peace, and joy
- Time of Angelic visitation (Zec 1:10-11/18-21), the miraculous and deliverance
- Time your prayers can literally shape the course of history. Even as Jesus made a triumphant covenant for us that we might live we must also take our respective cross to Calvary.

It is amazing how we as believers desire spiritual blessings and even spiritual breakthrough yet we seek God with a quarter of our hearts and expect full blessings in return. Lord let us, your bride awaken to the glory of prayer in a depth unheard of in the spirit of grace, supplication, prayer and intercession.

Psalm 61: 1-2 "Hear my cry, Oh God; attend unto my prayer. From the end of the earth will I cry unto thee, when my heart is overwhelmed: lead me to the rock that is higher than I."

Fasting & The Word

"Blessed is he that readeth…" (Rev 1:3 KJV)

The scripture says, we are already blessed just by reading the word of God. You will find that in the natural the less you eat, the more hungry you become. In the kingdom of God, the opposition holds true, the more you eat the word of God, the more hungry you become.

"Man shall not live by bread alone but by every word that proceedeth out of the mouth of God" (Luke 4:4 KJV)

During fasting you quite frankly, pig out on the word of God. Think about those times in the natural that you eat and are not even hungry. Follow that seem principle. Eat when you are hungry during the fast and also when you're not. If you are an avid reader, you won't have much of a problem but for those that do not like reading, baby you are about to acquire the taste of the word. Oh taste and see that the word of the Lord is good.

I have found that when you take that extra quality time and spend feasting on the word of God, you literally start to see hidden secrets kept in the word for you at the appointed season you are in. Your understanding is enlightened radically as words start to pop out at you, or become illuminated on the page as you read. You will begin to have revelation of Jesus Christ as He reveals more of His divine nature to you through His word. The Holy Spirit will teach you things and have you to learn things that will impress and astound others because you got them from the eternal of God. He is the omniscient one and when we go to Him and sit at His feet, knowledge beyond this natural realm is accessible to us. The prophet Isaiah says he will give you the tongue of the learned (50:4 KJV).

The more of the word you have in your spirit, the more armed and dangerous you are against the Kingdom of darkness. The sharper the blades of your double edged sword that can cut and divide asunder. There is hidden manna (Revelation 2:17) in the word that's waiting on you to search out. It is available every day. "Give us this day our daily bread." Fresh revelation.

2 Samuel 22:31 (KJV) "As for God, His way is perfect; the word of the Lord is tried: He is a buckler to all them that trust Him."

Psalm 33:4 (KJV) "For the word of the Lord is right."

Psalm 103:20 (KJV) "Bless the Lord, ye His angels that excel in strength, that do His commandments, hearkening unto the voice of His word."

Psalm 119:11 KJV "Thy word have I hid in my heart that I might not sin against thee."

Psalm 119:17 KJV "Deal bountifully with thy servant that I might keep thy word."

Psalm 119:25 KJV "....Quicken me according to thy word."

Psalm 119:28 KJV "....Strengthen me according to thy word."

Psalm 119:38 KJV "Establish thy word unto thy servant who is devoted to thy fear."

Psalm 119:58 KJV "I entreated thy favour with my whole heart, be merciful unto me according to thy word."

Psalm 119:81 KJV "…I hope in thy word."

Psalm 119:101 KJV "I have refrained my feet from every evil way, that I might keep thy word."

Psalm 119:105 KJV "Thy word is a lamp unto my feet and a light unto my path."

Psalm 119:116 KJV "Uphold me according to thy word, that I might live and let me not be ashamed of my hope."

Psalm 119:133 KJV "Order my steps in thy word and let not any iniquity have dominion over me."

Psalm 119:169 KJV "....Give me understanding according to thy word."

Proverbs 13:13 KJV "Whoso despiseth the word shall be destroyed: but he that feareth the commandment shall be rewarded."

Eccl 8:4 KJV "Where the word of a King is, there is POWER."

Is. 40:8 KJV "The grass whithereth, the flower fadeth but the word of our God shall stand forever."

Is. 55:11 KJV "So shall my word be that goeth forth out of my mouth: it shall not return unto me void, but it shall accomplish that which I please, and it shall prosper in the thing whereto I sent it."

Heb 4:12 KJV "The word of God is quick and powerful and sharper than any two edged sword, piercing even to the dividing asunder of soul and spirit and of joints and marrow, and is a discerner of thoughts and intents of the heart."

James 1:21 KJV "Wherefore, lay apart all filthiness and superfluity of naughtiness, and receive with meekness the engrafted word which is able to save your souls.

1 John 2:5, Rev 3:10, Rev 12:11

Fasting & Spiritual Warfare

"And I looked, and rose up and said unto the nobles, and to the rulers, and to the rest of the people, Be not ye afraid of them: remember the Lord, which is great and terrible, and fight for your brethren, your sons, and your daughters, your wives and your houses. " (Nehemiah 4:14 KJV)

One night during a fast the Holy Spirit said "**Fasting is Fighting**". Immediately I awoke and wrote that down. It is war time! Make no mistake about it, Fasting "precipitates a demonic showdown". Take out your armour, weaponry and suit up. The Apostle Paul provides us with the armour in Ephesians and commands us to

"Put on the whole armor of God, that ye may be able to stand against the wiles of the devil. For we wrestle not against flesh and blood but against principalities, against powers, against the rulers of the darkness of this world, against spiritual wickedness in high places" 6:11-12 KJV).

Each piece of the armour is detailed and significant and I will tell you why.

Loins – Girt about with **TRUTH**

Breastplate – **RIGHTEOUSNESS**

Feet – Shod with preparation of gospel of **PEACE**

Shield – **FAITH**

Helmet – **SALVATION**

Sword of the Spirit – **WORD OF GOD**

Prayer – In the **SPIRIT**

    * Now take each part and put it on

When we put this armour on, we literally clothed/cover our self with Christ Jesus. Jesus is our armour. Here we see how "The name of the Lord is a strong tower where the righteous runneth into it, and are safe" (Prov. 18:10 KJV). You are now "in the secret place of the Most High and abiding under the shadow of the Almighty" (Psalm 91:1 KJV- Emphasis mine). Have you noticed that Jesus is the **Truth**, He is our **Righteousness**, the prince of **Peace**, our **Faith**, the God of our **Salvation**, He is the **Word** and He is a **Spirit**. On our own, we are no match for the devil but when we are covered in the blood of the lamb and advance In Christ Jesus, the devil is no match for God. Once we now lift up this gate, the King of Glory comes in and He is the Lord strong and mighty in battle. He is the Lord of Hosts.

As you humbly seek and afflict your soul to diligently pursue the Lord, He will begin to reveal secrets from eternity to you. "The secret of the Lord are with them that fear Him and He will show them His covenant" (Psalm 25:14 KJV)

God uses ordinary people to accomplish extraordinary things! The gospel according to Luke says we have been authorized to legally use the power of God to trample serpents and scorpions (ch 10:19 KJV). We must now be tactical and strategic in this war. Ignorance and deception are tools the enemy uses to ensnare us. You are not warring against people. There are spirits behind those people that do not want you to be established nor establish God's kingdom. You can't play with the devil, you must slaughter him. Totally annihilate him from your person, home, family, city, island, state, or nation. It is War Time.

If you have dabbled in any of the following dark art areas and are about to fast, now is the time to renounce your involvement into these occult activities. Say this prayer:

Father, I confess my sins in _____ and humbly ask for your forgiveness for you are faithful and just to forgive me of all unrighteousness. I renounce my involvement in _____ and I repent on behalf of my forefathers back to my 5 and 6 generations participating in these activities. I break every and all demonic covenants, pacts, treaty and oaths made right now in the mighty name of Jesus Christ. I sever every tie, soul tie, spiritual tie, mind tie and break every cord, strap, hook, tentacle in my life now in the mighty name of Jesus Christ. Every seedling, egg, residue left in my spirit, soul and body, I call for the fire of the Holy Ghost to utterly consume you now. Right now. Lord I close up all the breach places in my spirit, soul and body and ask that your shed blood cover me, shield and protect me from the enemy. Galatians 3:13 says I am redeemed from the curse of the law. Today, I declare that you are my God and in you do I hope and trust. I commit myself solely to you. Use me for your honour and glory in Jesus' matchless name I pray. Amen.

**Now burn up all books, items, objects, charms, pendulums, rings, mixtures, powders associated with these activities

-Horoscope Reading

-Gambling

-Oujia Board

-New Age Movement

-Transcendental meditiation/Eastern Meditation

-Channeling

-Yo ga

-Levitiating

-Séance

-Witchcraft

-Vodoo

-Black/White Magic

-Santerio

-Pyschic/Spiritists

-Abortion

- Palm Reading
- Automatic Writing
- Water Witching
- Sorcery
- Satanism
- Necromancy
- Beastiality
- Voyerism/Viewing Pornography
- Astrology
- Divination
- Fortune Telling
- Interpreting Omens
- Soothsaying
- Talisman
- Chanting/Charms
- Idolatry
- Poltergeists
- Mediums
- Hypnosis
- I Ching
- Esp (Extra sensory perception)
- Astrol Projection
- Reincarnation

-Dungeons & Dragons

-Crystals

-Insubordination to authority: Pastors, Bosses, Parents

The reason this process is so specific, is because you can fast all you want but if these spirits are not expelled and the doors to them, closed, you will not experience full breakthrough. The need to consult the unknown or a higher supernatural being has been placed in man because "eternity has been placed in our hearts". Material things, a job, career or even degrees and titles even though good, will not fill the void that most feel, only the Lord can do that. Hence, the reason we seek the true meaning of life spiritually. As firm disciples of Jesus Christ, we consult the Holy Spirit who is the Spirit of Truth and of Grace. He is a revealer of secrets and will tell us things to come. We inquire only of the Lord. His promise is that his ears would be open and attentive unto our cry (1 Peter 3:12 KJV) and that He would show us great and mighty things we know not of (Jer 33:3 KJV).

Fasting & The Prophetic

Joel 2: 29 (KJV) says "And it shall come to pass afterward, that I will pour out my spirit upon all flesh; and your sons and your daughters shall prophesy, your old men shall dream dreams, your young men shall see visions".

Dear reader, we are living in a prophetic hour. The "Prophetic" anointing is very attractive, exciting, it is also incredibly challenging at times and can be extremely dangerous to the prophetic novice. You would note in scripture that ALL the prophets had a common thread and similarity of Fasting. This practice is crucial because the Prophet's voice is literally representative of the voice of God.

There are four divisions of prophesy or prophetic realms. This is necessary to understand so that we properly place ourselves and follow the movement of the Holy Spirit.

1. The Word of God. The sure word of Prophesy. It is infallible and incorruptible and stands forever.
2. The Gift of Prophecy. Corinthians 12:10. This can be stirred up as in 2 Timothy 1:6. The person ministering is confined to exhortation, comfort and edification (1 Corinthians 14:3). Venturing out beyond those guidelines can be destructive to the person ministering and to the lives encountered.
3. The Spirit of Prophecy. Upon entering the atmospheres of Prophets, during intense or high levels of worship or as the Holy Spirit wills, the Spirit of Prophecy can fall. Any believer can have the Spirit of Prophecy fall on them and begin to prophesy. It is done by the proportion of faith in the individual (Romans 12:6). This is limited by the word of God. The more word one knows, the easier the flow.
4. The Office of the Prophet. One of the ascension gifts (1 Corinthians 12:28). This is the highest realm of the Prophetic. Prophets have stronger utterances because they speak by the word of God, the Spirit of Prophecy, the Gift of Prophecy and from the strength of their office. They have the authority to go beyond the realm of exhortation,

edification and comfort and minister with a wider prophetic view. Prophets walk in the length, depth, height and width of the Prophetic realm. This is done under proper covering/leadership, decency and in order.

The prophet or prophetess is one of the fivefold ministers or ascension gifts listed in Eph. 4:11 (KJV). Prophets and prophetic people, those operating in the gift of prophecy and under the spirit of prophecy release the mind of God for people, islands, towns, provinces, cities and nations and generations to come. The Hebrew word for prophet in the Old Testament is "Nabiy'". Which translates spokesman, speaker actuated by a divine spirit. The Greek word in the New Testament is "prophetes" which means:

- An interpreter or oracles of hidden things
- One who speaks forth, announces or make known
- One moved by the Spirit of God who solemnly declares to men what was received by divine inspiration, especially concerning future events, in particular relating to the kingdom of God and to human salvation.
- Foretellers of deeds and deaths
- Men filled with the Spirit of God who by God's authority and command in words of weight plead the cause of God and urge men to salvation
- They are associated with Apostles
- Have power to instruct, comfort, encourage, rebuke, convict and stimulate their hearers

Prophets have the supernatural ability by virtue of the grace of God on their lives to perceive, sense, see and direct God into prosperity. To also release a building and a finishing grace or anointing upon a people (Ezra 6:14). Prophets are very much "lone rangers". Not so much anti social but we enjoy quiet times and solitude so as to always be in tune with the Holy Spirit. Prophets are keepers and carriers of the law of God. Prophets stand in the eternal counsel of the Lord and are intercessors by nature. Every true prophet has a vibrant, fervent and consistent prayer life. Not all intercessors though are prophets. Through much prayer and fasting, your prophetic senses will be trained by nullifying or killing the flesh. According to Dr. Cindy Trimm in her book

"Prophets And Prophecy", our 5 senses will be trained and exercised in the prophets life to discern both good and evil (Hebrew 5:14).

5. Visual. Fasting releases new insight, foresight and vision for the Prophet. Jeremiah 4:16/Ephesians 1:17-18
6. Auditory. Our hearing is fine tuned to the correct frequency and band of the Holy Ghost. We must not just pray but we should also practice the art of listening and sometimes being still before the Lord, especially after a time of prayer. Revelation 2:29
7. Gustatory. Our spiritual receptors and antenna are sharpened and heightened. Psalm 34:8/Jeremiah 1:4-9/Revelation 10:8-11
8. Olfactory. Our sense of smell or discernment is developed with accuracy. Hebrews 5:13-14
9. Kinesthetic. Our feelings, stirrings and promptings by the Holy Ghost become more than strong, but unshakable and on point. Exodus 35:21

Information received from the Holy Spirit can be translated or communicated prophetically in many different forms: some prophets minister only by the written word of God, some use the rhema word of God, others use prophetic acts and demonstrations. Regardless of method, we must understand that all things are done by the counsel of HIS will.

True prophets always point people to Christ Jesus and not to themselves. Prophets are messengers and delivery agents. If you are reading this book and turned to this chapter before any other, you are prophetic in nature. Never get to the place where you start saying "I said" or "I prophesied". Suggestion, use "the Holy Spirit ministered through me" or some say "thus saith the Lord" or "hear the word of the Lord". Lose the I, me and self. Because it was never about you and when it starts to be about you, it ceases to be about God. We want all the glory and honor to be the Lord's.

Fasting flushes our spiritual pipes, helps to remove or point to blockages and fine tunes our hearing in the realm of the Spirit. For the prophet, fasting helps to keep us humble as well by putting our flesh in subjection to the spirit of the Lord. Our spiritual eyesight is corrected and perfected as we spend this intense and quality time with God. Honestly, many are attracted to the prophetic but are not willing to pay the price to carry this anointing. As with the other ascension gifts, the prophetic is a very peculiar anointing because many times prophets undergo great hardship and suffering as examples of the word and to be able to perfect our faith. Are you willing to pay the price today? When you see a prophet ministering in front of a crowd or to a believer, that person has literally been through the fire with God to be used as an authentic voice or an oracle of God. I heard a quote one day that said "the strength of an oak tree is not in its branches, but in its roots." You pay a hefty price behind the scene to have roots grow and go deeper because for many years sometimes, your life and ministry is in obscurity so that you plunge deeper in wells of love, sink into depths and dimensions of revelations and interpretation in the spirit towards God. But if you would pay the price, you will be like an oak tree that last for hundreds of years and is a precious material to the carver or carpenter which is Christ Jesus.

Prophecy is given for edification, exhortation and for comfort. The well of prophecy flows in the current of love, at low tide or high tide. Love is the bases for all prophetic utterances. Prophets, yes are known for what they speak coming to pass but a real Prophet is known by fruit not just on the basis of his gifting. Jesus said John the Baptist was the greatest Prophet and he never worked one miracle or gave some profound prophetic word. However, he did in spirit and in truth prepare the way for Christ. Authentic prophets prepare the way for the Lord.

Benefits & Blessings of Fasting

Oh reader this is one of the most exciting chapters you will ever read in any book. I am bursting with joy even as I write. In 2010 as I was compiling information for a message on Fasting, the Lord showed me this specific topic was to be published: **The Benefits & Blessings of Fasting.** One of the Pauline epistles says that "God is a rewarder of them that diligently seek Him" (Heb 6:11 KJV). It is impossible to go before the King of Glory and not leave without His **Glory** upon you. The book of Psalms talk about how in His presence is fullness of joy and at his right hand there are pleasures forevermore (chapter 16:11 KJV). Now that should get you serious about fasting. Personally, I have never fasted and not been rewarded. I've gotten things I didn't even request, and definitely according to man's standards were not qualified for.

Expect any and or all of the following:

From Isaiah 58

- Light –Revelation, Illumination, knowledge, ideas, inventions
- Health – Shall spring forth speedily
- Glory – Resources, favour, honour, dignity
- Righteousness – Justice, vindication, salvation
- Answered Prayer: Jer. 33:33 (KJV)
- Interpretation of Dream(s)
- Divine Direction & Guidance – Cleared Pathway
- G.P.S. (God Positioning System)
- Influence
- Satisfaction
- Refreshing & Rejuvenation
- Work That Endures
- Restoration – Marriage, children, parents, work, etc.
- Supernatural Strength
- Signs, Wonders & Miracles
- Casting Out of Demonic Spirits

- Divine Revelation
- Intensifies Your Anointing
- Purifies Your Spirit
- Enlightens the Soul
- Sharpens Spiritual Sight & Hearing
- Activates Spiritual Gifts
- Accelerates Spiritual Growth
- Divine Intervention
- Breaks bad habits & cycles
- Destroys Yokes
- Destroys generational curses
- Undo Heavy Burdens
- Looses soul ties
- Prepares you for spiritual warfare
- Accessibility of authority of Demons
- National repentance, cleansing and prosperity
- Helps us to be disciplined
- Promote order & structure in our lives
- Increases sensitivity to the Holy Spirit
- Creates a closer bond with Father
- Builds Confidence & Faith In God
- Raises our own self esteem & self worth
- Money/Opportunity/Door Opened
- Supernatural Prosperity
- Wealthy Place locater
- Salvation of souls
- Identification of Hindrances
- Removal of Blockages
- Promotion & Elevation both spiritually & Naturally
- Exposition of Weak Areas that need to be corrected
- Loss of Weight
- Detoxifies the body
- Healthy & Younger Skin
- Acute Spiritual & Mental Agility & Ability
- Reveals Purpose & Identify
- Clarifies Assignment
- Provides mode of operations
- Cutting Edge Strategies & Maneuvers
- Shields us from impending danger
- Curb unhealthy appetites

One day during a fast the Holy Spirit prompted me to go and look for a lady who visited my church. When I saw her she immediately told me how she was praying to see me because her son's girlfriend was over 10 months pregnant and she wanted me to pray for her as it was an unnatural occurrence. I told her to bring the lady to prayer meeting that night and she did. I was instructed to place my hands on her womb and speak life over the unborn child and call it forth. She delivered a healthy baby girl within 24 hrs. God wrought a mighty miracle. During another fast, an elderly gentlemen came to our midday service that needed sight. The Lord gave me a word of knowledge to pray for his eyes and immediately he started to see some stuff. I prayed 2 other separate times and each time the gentleman received clearer sight. There was yet another time the Spirit of the Lord had me to prophesy to a gentleman that he would win his court case and he did. So you will not be the only one benefitting and blessed by fasting but those around you as well.

If you are reading this book there is something you need from this expansive list not today, like yesterday. Put God to the test and He will indeed show "the exceeding greatness of His power to usward who believe according to the working of His mighty power" (Eph. 1:19 KJV) above and beyond what you could ever ask or think. It is not just your time, it is your turn! I Dare you!

"That in the ages to come, He might show the exceeding riches of His grace in His kindness toward us through Christ Jesus (Eph. 2:7 KJV)".

Fasting & The Day Of Atonement

The "Day Of Atonement" or Yum Kippor is known as the most holy and sacred day in the Jewish Calendar. This is a fixed time, an appointed meeting that Father has ordained to meet with His people. On this day, which is a Sabbath as well, the Jews and those disciples of Jesus Christ gather in synagogues, temples and or sanctuaries to worship the Lord God Almighty. This day begins from Sundown on the Friday before to sunset on the Sabbath. Jews and disciples of the Lord do a self introspection repenting of our sins of rebellion and wickedness and thanking the Lord for taking our place to be slaughtered. It is said that our fate for the next year is decided as God opens the book of life on us and grant us certain inheritance for the new year. Jews believe the destiny of each believer hang in the balance in heaven's courtroom as we stand trial and await a verdict on this holy day. During this time, we afflict or humble our souls with fasting and prayer before the Lord. This is the only time in the entire Bible that we are <u>commanded to fast</u>. It's not our option. It is a clear directive. At this time we acknowledge Christ's work on the cross, our redemption, santification and perfection (Hebrews 10).

The Day Of Atonement and all other feasts are ordinances and are to be kept from year to year as a memorial before God. The Gregorian calendar was established because the Jews prospered as a result of observing these specific times and seasons and the enemy wanted to hinder or stop growth, success and progression. But thanks be unto the Lord for the Holy Ghost, our Teacher and bearer of truth. I first started observing these Feasts about 3 years ago. The first year, my brother and I both observed the Day of Atonement; but he sowed a greater seed than I did. Both of us got property released to us but he paid 0 dollars for legal or surveying fees while on the other hand I had to pay for legal services. There are no favourites in God. We are rewarded in the measure of our obedience. I was granted my portion, but because his level of sacrifice exceeded mine, his reward did as well. That brings me to another important point. On "The Day Of Atonement", we go before God with an Atonement or a Tresspass offering (Ex. 23:15/Lev 23:8). Never, ever appear before the King of Kings empty handed. You wouldn't even think to do that naturally. How much more so our heavenly king? It is said that our sacrificial offering acts as a symbol of Atonement for our household and family and literally "covers" or "removes" and forgives our sins as Jesus Christ died and was the lamb of God slain on our behalf. It must be noted however, it has absolutely nothing to do with your money but everything to do with us honouring God and respecting heavenly palatial protocol. No amount of money we could ever amass or offer can wash away our sins (and some of us have sinned enough for generations)......For it has already been done. Praise the Lord! Where a man's treasure is, there will his heart be also. Your sacrificial offering displays the state of your heart, the position of your spirit and the nature of your soul towards God. Whatever you give, give it cheerfully, not grudgingly that it may be respected and received by the Lord.

This is a kairos moment in God when divinity comes down and impacts or changes your humanity. When there is a touch down from the God of eternity into time. There is a literal ripping and opening in the heavens. Hence, the Atonement season has an Atonement portal, window, opening, channel that's created for your benefit and blessing.

The Blessings & Benefits of Observing The Day Of Atonement

1. There is a divine outpouring of God's presence in your life. Lev. 26:11/Is 58

2. Time of spiritual and soulical cleansing and sanctification. Ex 16:30

3. Household Deliverance & Salvation. Lev. 16:11 & 17

4. An angel will be sent ahead of you to take you to the place God has ordained and prepared for you. Supernatural Escort and divine assistance Ex 23:20.

5. Father will send his fear ahead of you and be an enemy to your enemies and an adversary to your adversaries. Ex 23:22 & 27. You shall see your enemies Fail and Fall before you. Lev. 26:7

6. Once you have put away idolatrous worship of false Gods, Father Promises that he will bless your bread and water and remove sickness away from your midst. Supernatural healing takes place. Ex.23:25/Is.53:5

7. Barreness will be removed from you. Productivity, multiplication and fruitfulness shall be your portion. Divine increase. Ex 23:26/Lev 26:9

8. Releasing of inherited land and or property prepared for you. Ex. 23:30. Experience increase of anointing, usage of giftings of the spirit, increase of fruits of righteousness, increase of revelation, increase of faith and favour, increase of authority and glory. Ez 36:11

9. Our heavenly Father will set your boundaries, borders, coasts whereby you shall have dominion over every evil spirit that once rose up against you. Sure promise of Peace & victory. Lev. 26:6/Ex.23:31/Ez. 34:28

10. Father will fulfill the number of thy days. Ex. 23:26

11. Father will break demonic bands and satanic yokes from off, over and around you. You shall experience a new level of liberty in every facet of your life. The liberty and strength to walk upright and truly please God is given at this time. Lev 26:13/Ez 34: 26, 27/Is. 10:27

For a deeper understanding, please do further research on this topic.

Daily Prophetic Declarations

1. In 2015, Lord let your Holy Fire, Passion & Zeal be unquenchable in and through my life.
2. I prophesy that this year my life, business, ministry, family, finances & destiny will know no LIMIT, BOUNDARY nor BORDER. Every satanic barrier of restriction be destroyed by Fire, in Jesus' name.
3. This year, the same God that destroyed the garments of shame and sickness from blind Bartimaeus shall do likewise in my life in Jesus' name.
4. I declare and decree that every evil, satanic and occultic power gathered to curse, block and stop me be destroyed by Fire now in Jesus' name.
5. I prophesy that every satanic blanket covering my Glory, catch a fire now in Jesus' name.
6. I command the elements: sun, wind, moon, stars, water and fire to all cooperate with me fulfilling my destiny.
7. The only tears I will cry in 2015 will be that of Joy & Gladness.
8. This year I am prophetically and apostolically aligned to my divine destination and poised for my supernatural allocation in Jesus' name.
9. I decree that 2015 is the year I am the exception to natural laws and the exemption to physical rules in Jesus' name.
10. I prophesy 2015 as my year of latter RAIN/REIGN. Money of all kinds & Favour with men will be magnetized to me from the east, west, north and south.
11. In 2015, those that once commonized me shall see my Sudden Rise and Canonize (reverence) me by reason of the anointing upon my life in Jesus' name.
12. I declare that 2015 will be the year my cup of MIRACLES, SIGNS, WONDERS & BREAKTHROUGH run over in Jesus' name.
13. I prophesy 2015 is my year for Manifestation and Celebration in Jesus' mighty name.
14. This year I declare that I shall taste and see the awesome power of God in every facet of my life.
15. In 2015, my name shall be associated with GREATNESS & GLORY and my life with UNCOMMON SUCCESS.

Life After Fasting

If you haven't experienced an all out attack on your fast, expect one now. Newsflash and red Alert: Expect the intensity and plateau of the attack to be almost mind blowing and heart throbbing. Experientially speaking, every time you fast, you gain ground and or territory in the realm of the Spirit. You forthrightly push the kingdom of darkness back and boldly advance the kingdom of God and the Devil is outraged. Just don't laugh too hard because he is coming after your jugular now. The beauty about completing a fast is you are strengthened with supernatural might in your inner man, whether you feel like it or not, and have been prepared for the day of battle. You must remember by way of the notes you took whilst fasting, what the Lord spoke to you, and ministered to your spirit through the word of God; and hold fast to your profession of faith without wavering. Spirits of retaliation, revenge, backlash, intimidation, manipulation, murder, slander and propaganda will not be on your trail but now in your face. The more they come, the more they will be scattered. "The harder they come, the harder they shall fall". Smile. The Spirit of the Lord will lift up a standard in you against the enemy. You are more than a conqueror already.

It will be essential to your new level of spiritual reality and maturity that you continue the walk of purity and integrity before the Lord. His word promises that "He preserves the life of the faithful".

It's one thing to fast but when the temptations start coming you will need to exercise your new found strength in making the right decision and the Lord will back you up. Don't play with it and don't linger when you know the right thing to do. Use the mind of God (word of God) and make the choice outlined for you in scripture in that situation. It is not always easy to make and do the right things because it literally crucifies our flesh but it gives joy and life to our spirit. The fact that you made it through this fast, you will make it past this hurdle. Victory is not the end thereof, but the process and journey you took to win the battle! Victory is undeniably yours. Shout unto God with a voice of Triumph! Glory!!!

Psalm 24

Some Tips

1. Make fasting a regular practice like once per week unless otherwise led by the Holy Spirit.
2. Be sensitive to the Holy Spirit's presence as you fast and afterwards. You want the presence of the Almighty God which increases during the fast to linger.
3. Believe that you have received that for which you fasted. You must see it done through the eye of faith.
4. Continue to repeat the Prophetic Daily Declarations until they naturally and forcefully pour out of your spirit. Stay in prayer and remember to pray for Jasmin Dareus Ministries & Kingdom Harvest Global Ministries, children and family.
5. Break your fast with soft food first, fruits then graduate to solid food around day three after fasting. This is to avoid abdominal cramps.
6. Read the word of God. Read the word of God and continue in prayer.
7. Refuse to murmur and complain. Dismiss doubt.
8. Wait on God and wait on your season in God.
9. Sow a financial seed at this time if you haven't during your fast. Especially if your fast was for a financial turn around and increase. You can make cheque/money order payable to:

Jasmin Dareus Ministries/Kingdom Harvest Global Ministries
P. O. Box F-44252
Freeport,
Grand Bahama,
Bahamas.

10 Laws Of Kingdom Alignment & Availment

The Ten Commandments – Our Moral Guidelines For Living

1. "Thou shalt have No other gods before me." Father is saying I must be the Supreme Being in your life. No other gods are to be placed before me; be it your house, car, children, job, spouse, business, money, etc…Nothing and no one else will satisfy.

2. "Thou shalt NOT make unto thee any graven image…" The Lord is a jealous God and rightfully so. We are not to make images or icons; we are to go directly to the Lord for He hath made us and not we ourselves.

3. "Thou shalt Not take the name of the Lord thy God in vain.." We must love God enough to respect His name. We are talking about the name whereby angels and the four and twenty elders cry "Holy, Holy, Holy, Lord God Almighty" and the name where things also in the earth and underneath the earth must bow to. This commandment is relevant and needed in our times. Let us only use the name of the Lord to reverence Him and bring Him Glory.

4. "Remember the Sabbath day, to keep it holy. Six days shalt thou labour and do all thy work: But on the seventh day is the Sabbath of the Lord: in it thou shalt not do any work, thou, nor thy son, nor thy daughter, thy manservant, nor maidservant, nor thy cattle, nor thy stranger that is within thy gates." To expound on this I will need another book all by itself. However, bear in mind that this is the only day that the Lord put a ***BLESSING*** on; He then went on to ***SANCTIFY*** (set it apart from the rest) it and called it ***HALLOWED*** (Holy). The Sabbath is designed to recreate and or provide us with the Garden of Eden experience of divine fellowship and intimacy. It is a day of rest, healing and finding our roots in God. We are called to <u>REMEMBER</u> the Sabbath day because centuries ago Father knew we would be busy about nothing and most likely our worldly responsibilities would cause us to forget it.

5. "Honour thy Father and thy Mother: that thy days may be long upon the land which the Lord thy God giveth thee." The First commandment attached to a promise. Consider, there is a divine relationship between health, long life, happiness and prosperity when we reverence/honour our parents. It doesn't matter if they did you wrong, Honour is a commandment that you must uphold. Maybe your biological parents have passed, then whoever Fathers and Mothers you should be respected.

6. "Thou shalt Not Kill." We are not to murder our fellow man, innocent men nor babies (Abortion). We are to remember that the gift of life comes only from God.

7. "Thou shalt Not commit adultery." Speaking loudly to our generation in a time of grave immorality and perverseness, here we are being called to walk in moral purity. It serves to free us from sexually transmitted diseases and calls us from physical, mental and emotional brokenness when we disregard the laws of purity and morality that has been instilled in the fabric of our being.

8. "Thou Shalt Not Steal." Don't Do It. This law serves to protect the possessions the Lord has given to us. It is wrong and yea even a sin to steal on every level: time from work, God, shoplifting, taking your neighbours fruit without permission.

9. Thou Shalt Not Bear False Witness against thy neighbor." Lying is still a sin. Gossiping and slandering someone's good name is wrong. This law serves to protect our dignity and reputation.

10. "Thou Shalt Not Covet." We are to be content with the blessings Father has given us. Focus on praising God for what you do have and don't complain about what you do not have.

The Ten Commandments were introduced as "I am the Lord thy God, which have brought thee out of the land of Egypt, out of the house of bondage." It is the Lord God, Elohim, the most High God, maker and creator of the heavens and the earth that wrote these commandments with His very own finger on tablets of stone as a moral principle for all times.

"The works of His hands are verity and judgment; all His precepts are sure. They stand fast forever and ever. He has commanded His covenant forever." Psalm 111: 7-9

"For this is the covenant that I will make with the house of Israel after those days, says the Lord: I will put my laws in their mind and write them on their hearts; and I will be to them a God and they shall be to me a people." Hebrews 8:10

Yes, beloved we are indeed under Grace. However, Grace only came to fulfill the law and not negate (refute/deny) it. Let us be governed thereby. Selah.

Conclusion

Fasting does not change God, it changes you! Fasting literally removes the paralysis and barrier of fear for you to arise in supernatural Faith to believe that with God ALL THINGS ARE POSSIBLE (Luke 1:37).

Sometimes you may be tempted to feel like God did not respond to your fasting or prayer and that counsel is directly from the enemy wanting you to walk by what you see. God promises He will answer when we come to Him in humility and affliction of soul. However, the answer may not be what you anticipated (Smile). Rest assured, He will answer you. Even if you don't see results on the first, second or third day, it is already done. The results or rewards from fasting may not be automatic, but they are assured!

You will never go into the King of Glory's presence and return without glory upon you. Glory being defined as honour, integrity, resources, favour, finances, affluence and influence . The Bible says it like this, as you delight yourself in the Lord, He gives you, He sets apart for you, He designates to you, He separates for you, and He apportions to you the desires of your heart (Psalm 37:4 KJV).

"Ask and it shall be given, seek and ye shall find, knock and the door shall be opened unto you. For everyone that asketh receiveth, and he that seeketh findeth, and to him that knocketh, the door shall be opened. Or what man is there of you, whom if his son ask bread, will give him a stone? Or if he ask a fish, will give him a serpent? If ye then being evil know how to give good gifts unto your children, how much more shall your father which is in heaven, give good things to them that ask of Him?" (Matt 7:7-11 KJV)

As you fast you will become acutely aware of the presence of the Lord on you and around you. You will also be able to identify others who have spent time fasting because when you get together there will be an intensity or an explosion of the Lord's presence. Some experience a tingling sensation all over their body or some electric shock. You may not feel anything but still unmistakingly aware of His strong presence. Your sensitivity spiritually will soar to unimaginable heights. Try to maintain this presence always. When we merely live with principles, we achieve some success but when we live and abide in

His presence, there is no failure. You will acquire the edge you need to excel and eliminate the demonic competitors. The only competition you are in is to be a better you than you were before. There is no competition for the man or woman who dares to live a life in the spirit and who is pleased to dwell under the shadow of the Almighty .

Today, you are ready to hold that which has been in your heart in your hands because your spirit and soul is crying out for a fresh move of God. Your greatest dreams, goals and aspirations are about to become a reality. You can and you will succeed not just in fasting but also in life. I am excited for you! The worst is over and the best is yet to come. The Benefits and Blessings of Fasting are now YOURS!

Appendix

Eight Proven Prayers For Manifestation constructed by Prophetess Jasmin Dareus

Child Bearing Prayer

I thank you Lord that I can come boldly before your throne of grace today and obtain mercy and find grace in the time of need (Heb. 4:16).

According to Psalm 51, Lord wash and purge me thoroughly from mine iniquity and cleanse me from sin. I declare that I am blood washed spirit, soul and body in Jesus' mighty name.

Lord create in me a clean heart and renew a right spirit within me. I present my body as a living sacrifice, holy and acceptable unto the Lord which is my reasonable service. I declare that this body is the temple of the Lord God. I decree that I am redeemed from the curse of the law (Gal 3:3)

Satan today you have been served eviction notice. According to (Luke 10:19) I have been given power to tread upon serpents, scorpion and nothing by any means shall harm me. Right now in the mighty name of Jesus Christ I command all generational spirits entered into my life during conception, in the womb, in the birth canal, through the umbilical cord, birth passage way and via blood to get out now. I break with the sword of the Lord all ill spoken words against my life, curses, hexes, vexes, jinx, incantation, chants, vows, potion, voodoo, black magic, white magic and witchcraft spirits in Jesus name. I also lay the sharp and powerful sword of the lord as stated in (Hebrew 4:12) to the root of strongman spirits in my spiritual and physical womb. Spirit of death, spirit of unfruitfulness, spirit of abortion, spirit of miscarriage, barrenness, witchcraft and sabotage spirit be destroyed by the anointing of the Holy One of Israel. I break every time release curse in my life and call null and void every demonic prophecy spoken against me and my family. I declare that every spiritual parasite feeding on the seed of my womb be destroyed. Die now in Jesus' name. Any evil plantation in my womb be uprooted and expelled right now by the fire of the Holy Ghost.

According to (Isaiah 54:17) No weapons formed against my conception, carrying and delivery of blessing shall prosper, and every tongue that rise up against me in judgment thou shalt condemn. This is my heritage as a servant of the Lord. The Bible declares whom the Son sets free, is free indeed. Thank you Lord that I am free, my spirit is free my mind is free and my womb is free for productivity and delivery in Jesus Mighty name. I cover my womb and reproductive organs in the blood of Jesus Christ.

Father, Jehovah Raffah, the great physician, correct any disorder in my ovaries, fallopian tube, womb, womb lining, walls, uterus. Surgically and super naturally right now reverse all irregular bleeding and I command regularity in Jesus name. I revoke the abnormal menstrual cycle and call you normal. Lord let your Holy Ghost Fire fall and utterly destroys demonic padlocks, chains, bolts and bars used to lock up, stop and hinder growth in my womb. Destroy them with your consuming fire tonight in Jesus' name. I close all doorways, gates, portals and entrances to the enemy in my life, I declare that all demonic eyes and SIB,FBI,CIA,INTERPOOL secret service surveillance to my pregnancy progress and success be blinded mute and paralyzed in Jesus' mighty name. Now every pain in my abdominal area, waist, beneath my belly I command you to cease and desist now in Jesus' name. Devil you will no longer devour the fruit of my womb in Jesus' name. I release into the realm of the spirit and prophesy that my womb is activated and ready for conception both physically and spiritually. Father, (John 10:10) states that you came that I might have life and have it more abundantly. I speak and release life into the spirit of my womb. I prophesy in accordance with your word abundant life right now in Jesus' name. Lord I declare and decree a creative miracle has taken place in my womb. (Gen 1:28) command me to be blessed, fruitful, multiply and replenish and have dominion the earth. I take my legal authority and dominion and command my wombs to be Blessed and to multiply. Womb, hear the words of the Lord, womb you are blessed and womb you shall multiply in Jesus' Mighty name.

Now Lord I thank you that I am blessed and my quiver is full of children.

- I declare that my children are an heritage of the Lord: and the fruit of the womb is His reward (Ps 127:3-5)
- According to Isaiah 8:18, my children will be for a sign and a wonder to the people.
- (Deuteronomy 7:12-15) Thank you that you love me, blessed me, multiply me and also bless the fruit of my womb. There is no barrenness in you Lord.
- I decree that my children are wise and bring me joy. (Proverbs 10:1)
- I declare my children are obedient because thus is pleasing to the Lord (Col 3:20)
- My children are like well- nurtured plants and like pillar carved to adorn a palace.
- Thank you Lord that my children shall be great and my offspring like grass of the earth (Job5:25).

- Thank you for establishing your covenant with my seed after me (Gen 9:9) and for giving them land (Gen 13:15)
- The other families and nations of the earth shall be blessed through my seed (Gen. 22:18)
- Thank you for setting up my seed and establishing their kingdom (2 Sam 7:12)
- Thank you that the seed of the righteous shall be delivered (Pro 11:21)
- My seed shall remain (Is 66:22)
- Thank you Lord for pouring your spirit upon my son (s) and daughter (s) (Joel 2:28)

Thank you that my seed is blessed and shall possess the gates of the enemy and be mighty in the earth (Gen 22:17). I vow to train up my children in the way they should go and when they are old they will not depart from it.

Lord I know that you say whatever I ask in prayer, believing I shall receive. Thank you for exceeding and going beyond my expectation great and mighty miracle working God. I seal this prayer in the blood of the Lamb of Jesus Christ. Lord your word is established in my life in Jesus' name. Amen.

Prayer Over Husband & Marriage

Lord I thank you for the opportunity to come before the mercy seat. I am ever grateful that you died and rose and are now seated at the right hand of the Father and are making intercession for me. I praise You because You are the great and terrible God and there is none like You.

Today I present my marriage before You. Father You said that what you're joined together let no man put asunder. I declare every architect and enemy of conflict and hostility in my home be paralyzed now in Jesus' name. Let every evil power trying to draw and redesign my marriage die in Jesus' name. Every form of household wickedness released in my home. Get out now in Jesus' name. I break up and break down every curse affecting my family in Jesus' mighty name. I stand to rebuke and resist every spirit of rejection, resentment, bitterness, frustration, exasperation, intolerance and impatience. I command that your hold be now loosed. Get out of my home. Now. Right Now. Every demonic maternal and paternal string break, pop and sever right now in Jesus' name. I declare that the wall of defense over my family be built and strong in Jesus' name. I declare healing over all sore and broken family relationship in Jesus' mighty name. Every seed and residue from hurt, offense, pain, adultery and abuse of any kind I command you to be expelled and utterly destroyed by fire.

James 5:16-The effectual fervent prayer of a righteous man/woman availeth much. Father I stand in the gap for my husband _____ before the throne today. Lord I pray that you would cover him with the blood of Jesus Christ from the crown of his head to the sole of his feet. **I prophesy over him and into his spirit that the kingly anointing and priestly anointing would arise and come forth in his life right now. (Repeat).** By faith I call those things that be not as though they are (Hebrews11:1). *Speak what you want to see* I call _____ saved, sanctified, delivered and filled with the Holy Ghost. I call for the sword of the Lord to uproot every form of blockage in his life. Uproot every tree of rejection, self-pity, despondency, deception, lying, procrastination, laziness, bitterness, loneliness, resentment and inferiority right now in Jesus' name. I call for the right hand of the Lord to pull down the demonic strongholds in his life in these areas in Jesus' name. Let every ungodly generational taproot be cut and pulled out of his blood line now in Jesus' name. I declare that all extra-marital relationships with other partners collapse and die right now. I block future ungodly relationships from occurring with my shield of faith and the blood of Christ Jesus. I arrest over _____ every spirit of gambling, alcoholism and rebellion, addiction and compromise. I disengage him from satanic host right now in Jesus' name. Every satanic force and generational curse operating in my husband, because the two are one flesh, I command you by the power invested in me the mighty name of Jesus' Christ to vacate his premises(temple) right now. Get out. Isaiah 59:19 – and when the enemy shall come in like a flood, Holy Ghost lift up a standard against him. God lift up standard against every oncoming attack in his life. Attacks of the mind, attacks against his finances, attacks against his sexuality, attacks against his will/emotions. I declare there is standard being lifted up even now. Every covenant of untimely death against my marriage be destroyed right now. Every demonic decree of marital failure be consumed by Fire. I announce and proclaim, My marriage shall live and not die. I prophesy, my marriage shall live and not die. The zoe life of Christ Jesus be over my home today in Jesus name.

I call _____ a Holy man, a righteous man, a worshipper, a lover of the things of Christ Jesus. He is a man of truth, a man of integrity; he is wise prudent, faithful, runs our home well in the fear of the Lord. I declare that my husband loves me, protect me and gives himself for me that he might sanctify and cleanse me with the washing of water by the word of God. He puts his family second only to God and first above all else. That he may present me to Yahshua in glory not having spot or wrinkle, a beautiful bride. I declare my marriage has agreement (Amos 3:3), love, unity, fire, passion, humour, togetherness and oneness. I present the foundation of our marriage back to you Lord because (Ps 127:1) says expect the Lord build the house, they labor in vain that build it. Build our marriage Lord on a sure foundation which is Christ Jesus. The foundation that is unshakable and immovable. Lord I thank you that my marriage is honorable and the bed is undefiled. Lord I declare that my husband has a new found love, passion and desire for me. His eyes only long to see this woman _____. I declare that my marriage is a testimony of your goodness and an example to others in the earth of the ultimate bride and groom relationship.

Lord I prophesy over _____.

According to proverbs 22:29: that his gift(s) will make room for him, he excel in his work and stand before kings.

Psalm 90:17 that you oh Lord will establish the work of his hands and whatsoever he doeth shall prosper.

A good man leaves an inheritance for his children's children. _____ is a good man and will leave an inheritance for his generation to come (Pro. 13:22).

I declare his walls are salvation and his gates praise (Is 60:18).

Lord that you are establishing him in righteousness (Is 54:14) and leading him in the path of righteousness for your name sake. (Ps 23)

I declare today as a sanctified wife, that my husband _____ mind is sanctified, his spirit is sanctified and his body is sanctified. I declare him this day off limit to the enemy and open to the moving of the Holy Ghost. That the eyes of his spirit be enlightened to know the hope of his calling. What the riches of the glory of his inheritance in the saints and what is the exceeding greatness of his power in him. (Eph 1:8)- That he may be able to know the love of Christ and be filled with the fullness of God.

I decree and declare it is so and call the zeal of the Lord of host to perform his word in Jesus mighty name (Isa. 9:7)

Prayer For Healing
Pray vigorously & passionately minimum 3x per day

Father, I come to you in the mighty, matchless, and omnipotent name of Jesus Christ, my resurrected Saviour and soon coming King. As an heir of salvation and joint heir with Jesus Christ, I stand in my legal dominion and God given authority as a son of God. According to Galatians 3:13, I am redeemed from the curse of the law and the law of sin and death has no power over me. I therefore refuse to suffer any longer from the powers of darkness. Father, I have been given jurisdictional authority over the enemy in the name of Jesus. The Bible declares that at the name of Jesus every knee must bow, of things in the heaven, in the earth and under the earth and every tongue must confess that you are Lord.

Right now, I declare every spirit of infirmity, disease, sickness, illness, infection illegal immigrants and are therefore trespassing on HOLY ground for my body is the temple of the Lord. Satan your hour, your season and time of operation in my life expires RIGHT NOW! Not tomorrow, nor next week, NOW in the majestic name of Christ Jesus. Every unlawful spirit your time of repatriation has come. Your demonic sentence, judgement, conviction, tariff, embargo, legality and technicality ends as of this moment. Now Devil. In the name of Jesus Christ every knee of sickness and infirmity in my life known or unknown bow:
List Of Diseases (Spirits)

- Liver disease
- Alzheimer's disease
- Amnesia
- Anxiety
- Anemia
- Arthritis
- Asthma
- Appendicitis
- Atopic Dermatitis
- Attention Deficit Disorder (ADD)
- Blindness
- Bronchitis
- Cataract
- Cellulitis
- Chronic Pancreatis
- Cirrhosis of Liver

- Chronic Renal Failure Depression
- Deafness
- Depression
- Eczema
- Fibroid
- Cancer: Lung, Breast, Prostate, Pancreas, Ovaries, Stomach, Brain, etc.
- Fibromyalgia
- Gall Stones
- Gastritis
- Gout
- Glaucoma
- Hay fever
- Hepatitis B & C
- Herpes
- Hyperthyroidism
- Irritable Bowel Syndrome
- Jaundice
- Kidney Stones
- Lipoma
- Lumber Spondilitis
- Migrane headaches
- Multiple Myloma
- Multiple Sclerosis
- Myasthenia Gravis
- Nasal Polyps
- Stroke & Angina
- Coronary Artery Disease
- Heart Murmur
- Mitral Valve Prolapse
- Osteoporosis
- Parkinson's Disease
- Peptic Ulcer
- Prostrate Enlargement
- Psoriasis
- Rhematoid Arthritis
- Sickle Cell Anemia
- Gonorreah
- Tuberculosis
- Sinusitis
- Vocal Nodules

- Warts
- Aids
- Diabetes
- Hypertension
- Lupus
- Viral Infections
- Bacterial Infections
- Citilamydia
- Scabies
- Paranoia

Matthew 15:13 says "Every plant which my heavenly FATHER hath not planted shall be rooted up." Infirmity, Sickness & Disease (call by specific name), you are plucked up out of place and rooted up from my life. Now pick up your weapons and flee. Get out now. You are evicted NOW! Flee out of my Skeletal system; get out of my neurological system; get out of my reproductive system, flee from my circulatory, endocrine and lymphatic systems now in Jesus' mighty name. You are officially bound, rebuked, released, expelled and loosed from my internal physical and spiritual organs. Every demonic entity living, hiding in my liver, spleen, ovaries, testacles, lungs, breasts, cervix, fingers, toes, abdomen, intestines, cranial structure, rectum, ureter, urethra, lymph nodes, nasal passage, auditory canal, iris, cornea, knee, shoulder, hips, tongue, gums, skin….. get out now. I arrest you and command your illegal activities in, on and around my system and organs to cease and desist now. I cancel every demonic telecommunication network, destroy geospatial intelligence and call forth a holy explosion on all taboo frequencies. I speak deafness, dumbness, & blindness upon all demonic traffic controllers, alliances, alternate authority and reconnaissance. The Fire of God be upon you now. Fire upon the enemy. I forbid and disallow any and all regrouping, counter attacks and retaliation troops in Jesus name. Every satanic and occultic contract operating in my life now be severed and terminated in Jesus' name. I call forth the south wind of the spirit now to blow and dry up the spirits of infirmity and disease in Jesus name.

Lord your word says you overthrow every hex, vex, incantation, potion, black magic, white magic, voodoo, witchcraft, chant, demonic prophecy against my health now in Jesus name. I call every power, work, curse of darkness concerning my health, healing and wholeness cancelled, null and void in the realm of the spirit and in the natural. Every power of the enemy, you are now defeated. I deploy the Blood of Jesus Christ over all of my systems and their respective organs. For "thou art my King O God, command deliverance for me today." (Psalm 44:4). I stand on and receive the WORD of GOD as my current and present reality. Your word is tried and true Lord.

I now prophesy according to Isaiah 53:5

"But He was wounded for our transgressions. He was bruised for our iniquities: the chastisement of our peace was upon Him; and with His stripes I am healed." Hallelujah…Hallelujah I am healed.

Psalm 34:19 says many are the afflictions of the righteous: but the Lord delivereth me out of them all.

Psalm 55:18 Lord you have delivered my soul in peace from the battle that was against me.

Lord I declare that you shall bless my bread and water and take sickness away from me. (Exodus 23:25)

I decree my bones are fat because I receive the good news/report of the gospel of Jesus Christ. (Proverbs 15:30)

I prophesy that my flesh shall be fresher than a child's and I shall return to the days of my youth. (Job 33:25)

Lord you shall renew my youth like the eagle's. (Psalm 103:5)

My beauty shall be as the Olive tree. (Hosea 14:6)

My soul shall not be cast down or disquieted within me for you, Oh Lord, you are the health of my countenance. (Psalm 43:5)

I thank you Lord that your healing virtue shall touch my life and heal me speedily in Jesus' name. (Luke 6:19)

Today Lord, I declare that you have risen over my life with healing in your wings. (Malachi 4:2)

I decree the Lord Is the Strength of my life (Psalm 27:1) of whom shall I be afraid? You are indeed my God that girdeth me with strength in my inner man.

Every plague is stopped because of the efficacious power of the blood of the atoned lamb named Christ Jesus the one from Nazereth (Luke 13:12)

I declare that it is Jesus Christ that makes me whole (Acts 9:34)

Lord today, you saw me polluted in my own blood and spoke to me and said "LIVE". (Ezekiel 16:6). Father I come into agreement with your word and I prophesy that I shall LIVE and not die to declare the Glory of the Lord. Life and death is in the power of my tongue and I choose LIFE today.

This day I eat your word for you are the bread of life. (John 4:13-14)

You have brought and delivered my soul from the pit Lord. (Jonah 2:6)

Today Holy & Righteous Father, your covenant with me is that of Life and Peace (John 6:48).

Today Lord, your spirit gives me life. For the words that you speak they are spirit and they are life. I speak and declare that I shall not only live but shall also have the abundant life promised in John 10:10.

Today most sovereign King and majestic Ruler, I freely drink and receive from the fountain of life. (Rev. 21:6-7)

Lord I have a right to the tree of Life because I do your commandments. (Rev 22:14)

For this very purpose was the son of God made manifest, that he might destroy the works of Darkness. Every work of darkness in the area of my health you are now destroyed by Fire for whom the son sets free, is free indeed.

Hallelujah. Hallelujah. Glory be to God. I seal this prayer in the blood and in the spirit with divine Apostolic and Prophetic authority and dominion. Be thou healed. Be thou set free in your body, soul and spirit. Every yoke of the enemy is now destroyed by the anointing. Be thou Healed in Jesus name. You have the victory. Shout Victory. In Jesus' name.

Amen. Amen.

Prayer For Ministers & Ministries

Father in the name of Jesus Christ, I come boldly before your throne of grace today. I bring before you (ministry name & or minister's name). Lord I acknowledge that I have been saved by grace and my calling is a gift from God. Your word says : Those whom you call, you also justify and those you justify you GLORIFY. I pray that as Jesus prayed, you would glorify yourself in me and through my ministry. Father, I earnestly pray for a new level of glory to hit my life and ministry now in the name of Jesus. Take me from faith to faith and from glory to glory.

I declare that I shall abound in the work of the kingdom. For you have already given me all things that pertaineth unto life and godliness. Despite the works of the enemy, I shall dwell in the courts of the Lord all the days of my life to behold the beauty of your tabernacle and to inquire in your holy temple.

Let divine and holy utterance be given unto me that I may make known the mystery of the gospel of which I am an ambassador in bonds (Eph. 6:19-20). Open now doors that no man can shut and close those doors that no man can open (Rev. 3:7). Make me to know according to your word in Ephesians 3:16-19, the height, the depth, the length, the breadth and the knowledge of your son Jesus Christ and the glorious riches of the inheritance which is in Christ Jesus.

Show me the working of your mighty power how to effectively "perfect the saints, work the ministry and edify the body of Christ." (Ephesians 4:12)

Grant unto me the ability to always declare your truth in love and have my speech seasoned with grace that it may minister life to the hearers. Father help me not to grieve nor quench the Holy Spirit but rather like your ministers of old, be led by, sensitive and subject to the Spirit of God in everything.

Renew now the spirit of my mind and let the mind of Christ be also in me.

For the Lord God is a sun and a shield. The Lord will give grace and glory. No good thing will you with hold from them that walk uprightly before you(Psalm 84). I beseech you Oh Lord. Send now help into the Vineyard (state your location). For the harvest is truly ripe but the labourers are few. Send forth now laborers to carry out and assist in the kingdom. Those that you have assigned to me, I now loose and summons them into position (pray fervently in tongues). I also thank you for loosing financial resources and supplemental help.

Today, I declare every gate of brass broken over my life and ministry (call by name) and every bar of iron I declare you cut in pieces over my gifts, callings, assignment and destiny now in the matchless name of Jesus Christ (Is. 45:2)

I decree every yoke of bondage and curse of my pre-decessors be broken off my neck now. I burst, shatter and tear/rip asunder all bonds in my life and ministry right now in Jesus' name (Jeremiah 30:8).

Every demonic, satanic, occultic and dark arm, bow, arrow, dart, grip, hold of the enemy fashioned and levied against my calling and ministry and destiny be destroyed by the sword of the Lord. Every subtle and secret demonic barrier, barricade, spirit of stagnation and limitation be ye lifted up NOW. Right now that the King of Glory come in (Psalm 24). Every Jericho wall that has been erected to keep me out of my divine destiny and wealthy place; I command you now to fall down before me that my path be made straight and every rough edge smooth. Every Pharoah and Goliath spirit that's hindering my greatness and the release of my God given potential be swallowed up in the red sea. I call hail stones and coals of fire to burn the enemy. Fire upon the enemy in Jesus mighty name. (Pray passionately in tongues for 5 minutes).

Every whorish woman, Delilah, and Jezebelic spirit assisgned as an open sepulcher to cause my ministerial demise, receive judgement by Fire in the name of Jesus Christ. Every spirit of pride, haughtiness, arrogance and idolatry which are abominations before you, Lord consume by your holy fire that I may be a vessel unto honor fit for the master's use.

I reject every curse of spiritual blindness, deafness, muteness, lethargy, procrastination, insubordination, disorder, rebellion and failure. I bind, break and rebuke their powers from operating in my life and ministry. They shall not function in no form or familiar spirit. I declare every garment of shame, disgrace and dishonor be removed far away from me now in JESUS' NAME. Where I was rejected, I shall be the honoured, selected and the preferred in Jesus' name. Every curse of financial failure over my life and ministry be broken NOW. RIGHT NOW in Jesus name!

I declare my ministry a brazen wall, a fortified city, an iron pillar in the earth. A force of light to push back the rulers of the darkness of this world and in the spirit.

Gates of hell, you shall not, you will not prevail against the church. Glory. Hallelujah!

I have been given power over all the powers of the enemy and nothing by any means shall harm me, my children, my spouse, ministry, my members, covenant partners, followers in Jesus name (Luke 10:19). I shall run through every demonic troop and leap over satanic walls. If I should fall, I will not be utterly cast down for the Lord will uphold me with the right hand of His righteousness.

This moment, I bind to myself the fruit of the spirit: love, joy, peace, meekness, temperance, longsuffering, gentleness, goodness and faith. I declare my name is associated with spirits of advancement, progress, and great success.

Lord it is you that giveth me the power to get wealth. Power to get wealth, identity, locate and find me now in the earth realm. Witty inventions, supernatural strategies, divine downloads, data and hidden secrets of the ages be opened up to me now in Jesus mighty name. I declare that I shall suck the breast of gentiles and the milk of Kings. I shall be the lender and not the borrower. I shall be above and not beneath. The head and not the tail. Lord you cause those you love to inherit substance and you fill their treasures. I declare wealth and riches shall be in the house of the Lord (state ministry) and in my house.

I declare and prophesy that my life and ministry reflects God's power, glory and the majesty of His Kingdom in the earth. Surely goodness and mercy shall follow me.

Today I announce and boldly declare that my life is hidden with Christ Jesus in God:
I am who God says I am. I am God's Anointed.
I am fully functional and operational in every gift of the Spirit because I have been quickened by the Spirit and now walk in the Spirit being led totally by the Spirit.
I abide in the True Vine.
I am a joint heir with Christ Jesus.
I have been redeemed and blood washed.
I shall not die but live to declare the glory of the Lord.
I can do all things through Christ which strengthens me.
I am more than a Conqueror.

Today, I am strong in the Lord and of good courage (Joshua 1:8).

I shall not fret because of evil doers neither be envious of the workers of iniquity for they shall soon be cut down as the green bay tree. Glory to God.
I shall bring forth fruit in my season and whatsoever I doeth shall prosper (Psalm 1)
I declare that I have power with God in the heavens and He that ruleth in the earth so whatsoever I bind on earth, shall be bound in heaven and whatsoever I loose in the earth shall be loosed in the heaven (Matthew 18:18).

According to Isaiah 61, I declare that power and anointing over my life:

"The Spirit of the Lord God is upon me; because the Lord hath anointed me to preach good tidings unto the meek; He hath sent me to bind up the broken hearted, to proclaim liberty to the captives, and the opening of the prison to them that are bound; to proclaim the acceptable year of the Lord, and the day of vengeance of our God; to comfort all that mourn."

Lord as I have spoken, I also believe that wherever the words of the King are, there is power. Let these words now run swiftly to accomplish and bring about the will of Yeshua Ha Mashiach, my Lord and Savior concerning my life and ministry in the name of Jesus Christ, the son of the living God.

I seal this prayer with the blood of Jesus Christ and call it done. Amen. Amen. Pray in the spirit for another 10 minutes

Prayer of Deliverance from Rejection

Father, in the awesome name of Jesus Christ I come boldly before your throne of grace to obtain mercy in time of need. Your word says in Hebrews 11:6, he that cometh to God must believe that He is and that He is a rewarder of them that diligently seek Him. Your word also says to seek ye my face and whole heartedly today Lord, I declare your face is what I seek.

"Oh Lord, have mercy upon me according to the multitude of thy tender mercies blot out my transgression. Wash me thoroughly from mine iniquity and cleanse me from sin. Purge me with hyssop, and I shall be clean: wash me and I shall be whiter than snow. Create in me a clean heart, O God and renew a right spirit within me (Psalm 51).

Galatians 3:13 says I am redeemed from the curse of the law and I refuse to suffer any longer from the powers of darkness. Jesus. Jesus. Yeshua, Ha Mashiach. I call the name that is above every other name given in the heavens, on the earth or under the earth and things therein must bow. I bind according to Matthew 18:18 every spirit of abandonment, rejection, fear, loneliness, pity, resentment, guilt, fear, depression, sadness, hurt, bitterness, unforgiveness, sabotage, anger, rage, discouragement, grief and shame from my life and loose them from their assignment. I command you spirits to evacuate my body right now in Jesus name. Get out of my will, emotions, spirit and soul. Your time has expired.

As stated in Luke 10:19, I have been given legal power and authority over you devil and you cannot harm me. Spirits operating in my sexual character, organs, emotions, mind, conscience, appetite, occupying my spine, stomach, respiratory organs, skeletal system, circulatory system, endocrine system, muscular system or any other part of my life come out right now. Take up your weapons satan and flee in Jesus' name. I lay the sword of the Lord to the root of every evil spirit and or tree, generational tap root in my life in Jesus' name. According to Psalm 29, the word of the Lord that breaks and shatters. According to Hebrews 4:12, I skillfully use the word of God that is quick, powerful and sharper than any two edged sword to root up, pluck up, overthrow and utterly destroy the seed and residue of the enemy in Jesus name. Now God of Elijah, the God that answers by fire, consume every illegal immigrant in my life with your Holy Fire. I declare every serpentine poison that has been deposited into my life, get out now in Jesus name. I flush you out with the blood of Jesus Christ. I break and crush the head and tail of serpent spirits(Python, Anaconda, Rattlesnake,etc). Every demonic covenant, oath, pact, treaty, agreement that has been made concerning me be destroyed by the anointing immediately. Any replica of me, or item representing me catch a Fire now. Right now in Jesus name. I take authority over and destroy with fire all curses issued against my life and destiny. Depart from me now in Jesus' name. Lord Proverbs 22:12 says you overthrow the words of the transgressor. Lord overthrow every hex, overthrow every vex, overthrow every incantation, overthrow every potion, black magic, white magic, voodoo, witchcraft, overthrow every chant, overthrow all satanic prayers and false prophecies of the evil and iniquitous workers levied against me now in Jesus' name. I cough you up and spit you out in the name of Jesus. Thank you for great deliverance because I am your anointed (Psalm 18:50) and for putting all things under subjection to my feet. Lord I receive my deliverance through the blood of Jesus Christ.

Now Lord, whom the son sets free is free indeed. I now thank you for the spirit of liberty. I thank you that I am now free to walk in the spirits of : aggressiveness, boldness, zealousness, willingness, obedience, creativity, ingenuousness, inventiveness, retentive mind, maturity, purity, holiness, righteousness, excellence, praise, thankfulness, worship, singing, quietness, humility, intercession, good judgement, repentance, kindness, meekness, temperance, self control and all the gifts of the spirit: wisdom, knowledge, faith, prophecy, healing, miracles, supernatural increase in every area and keen discernment.

I declare and decree that no weapon formed against me shall prosper and every tongue that riseth up in judgement against me I condem (Isaiah 54:17).

I take my shield of faith to quench every fiery dart of the enemy (Ephesians 6:16).

I declare and decree that I am established in righteousness, and oppression is far from me (Isaiah 54:14)

I declare that I am blessed with all spiritual blessings in heavenly places in Christ Jesus (Ephesians 1:3).

I do not have the spirit of fear but of power, love and a sound mind (1 Timothy 1:7)
Lord thank you for anointing my head with fresh oil and allowing my cup to run over. Goodness and mercy shall follow me all the days of my life (Psalm 23:5-6).

I dwell in the secret place of the most High God and abide under the shadow of the Almighty (Psalm 91:1).

No evil will befall me and no plague come nigh my dwelling (Psalm 91:10)

I am strengthened with might by His Spirit in my inner man. (Ephesians 3:16)

I am rooted and grounded in love (Ephesians 3:17)

Now Lord thank you for not only hearing but also answering my prayer and for showing me great and mighty things. In Jesus' powerful name I pray. Amen

I seal this prayer and call it done. Amen. Amen

Prayer of Deliverance from the Spirit of Perversion

Father, I come boldly before you're throne of grace that I may obtain mercy in the time of need. According to your word, I am a new creation; old things are passed away and everything became brand new in my life. Lord, I thank you for the blood of Jesus to cover my mind, body and spirit. Now Lord, I thank you for the word of God to renew my mind and cleanse my ways enabling me to walk pleasing in your sight.

Today, I declare and decree all generational curses of pride, rebellion, stubbornness, lust, poverty, rejection, witchcraft, idolatry, molestation, incest, rape, sexual immorality, sickness, infirmity, disease, fear, bad luck, destruction, failure and death be smashed to dust now with the rock of ages and blown away by the Spirit of the living God. I employ the sword of the Lord and in the anointing and power of prophet Jeremiah chapter 1, I root out, pull down, pluck up break out and utterly destroy every tree that has been planted in my life by the enemy. I call for the fire of the Lord to locate and consume every and all seedling in my mind, spirit, soul and body immediately.

I arrest every generational or genetic curse, and or spirit operational and functioning in my life right now and bind them in fetters and chains. I refuse to be a victim and host to these spirits and therefore loose myself now from the spirit of perversion, adultery, fornication (in my hips, eyes, fingers, feet, abdomen, genetalia), spirit of uncleanness, seduction, sexual fantasy, sexual addiction and sexual immorality (eyes, thighs, hips, lips, tongue, legs, genetalia, mind). I command all of the aforementioned spirits to get out of my sexual character, sexual organs, sexual appetite, abdomen, out of my blood and neurological system, get out of my groin and loin areas right now in the name of Jesus Christ. Get out now in Jesus name. Every spirit of guilt, shame, intimidation, low self esteem, manipulation and condemnation associated with your presence, flee now, go now in Jesus name. Every sexual serpent spirit that have twisted and coiled around my sexual charater, spine, neck, bones, limbs, mouth, ears, eyes, (list your own condition), I release the rod of God to swallow up every sexual, seductive, sensual serpent spirit (Exodus 7:12) in the name of Jesus. Satan I crush your power and trample you under my feet. Now loose my sexuality, loose my spirituality and let me go free. Loose me now devil in Jesus' name.

Every door, gate or entry point that I have opened through sexual promiscuity, adultery, fornication, molestation, homosexuality, bestiality, rape and sexual impurities of all kinds; I now close the doors shut and every gate locked and I forbid you entrance into my mind, soul, body and spirit. Every ungodly soul tie with past boyfriends, married men, women, friends and or family members. I loose and break the ties now in the omnipotent name of Christ Jesus. Every signed sexual contract and covenant written in the underworld, I obliterate it, cancel and nullify it now. As of today, spirits of incubus and succubus you are forbidden to enter my realm and space in Jesus name. I declare your works and power over my life destroyed today. The Bible declares whom the son sets free is free indeed. Father, I declare liberty, liberty, freedom, freedom in the realm of the spirit from every demonic work of darkness concerning my sexuality.

I now loose all spirits of double mindedness, mind control, mental illness, memory recall, arrogance and disobedience from my mind and will and command them to never return in Jesus' name. I furthermore command every form of spiritual, sexual transmitted diseases to disappear or dissipate; be flushed out of my body which is the temple of the Lord right now. I declare my spiritual and physical immune systems strengthened, restored and healed right now (Psalm 119:28).

Every covenant or contract of death over my life and lineage I dissanul and cancel by and with the blood of Christ Jesus, and the word of God. I speak life over my body, life over my spirit and life over my soul in Jesus' name.

I declare according to Galatians 3:13 that I have been redeemed from the curse of the law.

I release myself and break myself loose from every and all curses be it from past heresies, breaking a person's heart, self imposed curses, involvement in false religion and the occult, tithe failure, deliberate sinning, word curses, erroneous prophecies and all negative words spoken over and in my life. I destroy bad habits, demonic cycles and spirits of failure, defeat and backward movement from over my life right now. I bind and rebuke along with loosing myself from spirits of laziness, procrastination, lethargy, insubordination, rebellion, spiritual retardation, malignant growth, stagnation and spiritual deformity in Jesus' name.

No more will the enemy triumph over me. Where there was failure, I speak and release divine success. All frustrations, turnaround now and become fulfilments. Where there was rejection, I thank you Lord for acceptance. Every pain be converted now to pleasure. There shall be no more poverty but plenty and prosperity be released according to my Father's good pleasure in my life. Where there were mistakes, turn now into messages and ministries in Jesus' name. Where there was sickness, be thou replaced with supernatural healing in Jehovah Raffah's name.

I declare that the anointing to excel locate, identify and fall upon me now in Jesus' mighty name. Every enemy of my advancement, progression, elevation and success I tread you under foot (Luke 10:19) and I crush your head with my heel. Devil I crush your head today. Every covenant made with the ground, water, wind, sun, moon and stars concerning myself be disarmed and cancel right now in Jesus' name. Amen.

All good things in my life that were dead or comatose, receive life right now. I command you to live. Life and death are in the power of my tongue; so you shall live in Jesus' name. Amen.

Every embargo, limit, tariff, sentence and ceiling placed on my giftings, talents, abilities, businesses, ministries and family be destroyed by the thunder and fire of God.

Every fake friend, destiny killer and illegal immigrant imposters, spiritual vultures masquerading around as genuine I declare you exposed. Speak the intent of your heart. Be disgraced and dispelled in the name of Jesus.

I declare every satanic judgement, decision, condemnation, conclusion and injunction against my life be nullified, destabilized in Jesus mighty name.

Amen.

Prayer for Financial Breakthrough

*After Fasting & Praying this prayer, my husband and I had a windfall of $40,000.00.

Resignation From Poverty

To the

Spirit of Poverty

Spiritual Rulers Of Darkness of Poverty

Spiritual Powers Of Poverty

Spiritual Principalities of Poverty

Spiritual Wickedness in High Places of Poverty

It is with great pleasure that I inform you officially and immediately of my departure from your strong hold of lack, inadequacy, frustration, insufficiency, not enough, and poverty. I hereby denounce your plans and call forth the Fire of Jesus The Almighty God, Yashua Ha Mashiach to rain down and consume your mandates and agendas in my life. I shut every door that I opened knowingly or unknowingly to you in the matchless name of Jesus Christ. I sever with supernatural, surgical precision with the sword of the Lord, every link, line, hook, entry, tentacle or access you had over my finances, homes, apartments, properties, shopping complexes, vehicles, businesses, yachts, planes, schools, employees, children and family members. My belongings are all covered, protected and guarded by Micheal and warring angels, the blood of the lamb of Jesus Christ, the Holy Ghost and the word of God. I now call forth money, prosperity, and wealth and riches to be within my house, my hands and swift recovery of every good thing that has been stolen, with held or have passed us by in the mighty name of Jesus.

I declare and decree right now. Now. Now. That the blood of Christ Jesus is assigned against every power of the enemy operating in my life in the following areas: money, finances, wealth, resources, income, land, inheritance, stocks, bonds, dividends, and income of every kind and from all sources and may the Blood of Jesus Christ speak for me. May the enemy hear the sound of the Blood and release the wealth of the wicked and all due finances and fruits of this and past seasons to me right now.

I bind and rebuke every delaying, hindering, entangling, interfering, cursed, bewitched, thieving, looting, plundering, devouring, every canker worm, palmer worm, locust, caterpillar, every foul, "jonesing" spirit against my money, prosperity and wealth in Jesus mighty name. With the scepter of Jesus Christ I decommission, dethrone, pull down, up root, castrate, paralyze, subdue, cancel, veto and nullify the spirit of poverty from my possession and inheritance. I bind up all satanic forces operating in the air, buried in the sand, planted in the earth, travelling subterraneous, sealed in buildings, linked to trees, plants and in grasses, transported in shipments, assigned generationally, genetically, martially or in any way connected to my wealth, health, prosperity, money, possession and inheritance.

I announce this day that I am a billionaire. I live to and stand on and speak forth that which is written of me in Deuteronomy 28: I am the head and not the tail. I am the lender and not the borrower, above only and not beneath. Landlords and not tenants. I am the righteousness of God through Christ Jesus. I therefore file an injunction in the court of the righteous judge for theft from royalty. I now command as stated in the Holy scriptures that you return back 7 fold for the seven dimensions of time stolen: every second, minute, hour, day, week, month, year and also (according to Prov. 6:30 KJV) give all the substance of hi house (shout with interest/increase) in the name of Jesus.

I speak and prophesy to the four winds of the earth (north, south, east and west winds) and command finances to now locate me in Jesus' mighty name. I call forth my prophetic portion, my prophetic Goshen to now be loosed in the name of Jesus Christ. I summons my apostolic ship laden down with goods and resources to complete my purpose and destiny that the Lord our God Jesus Christ has placed over my life to further His kingdom here on earth. I declare my prophetic gold, prophetic frankincense and myrrh to locate me now in Jesus name. I declare that I am dwelling and excelling in my wealthy place. As of today, I am walking in the Jabez anointing, the Abrahamic anointing, the Davidic anointing, the Cyrus anointing, the Isaachar anointing, the Joseph anointing, Solomon's anointing and the 7 fold edenic anointing.

You Lord said I shall be filled with the fruit of my lips and that I shall have what I say. I say today:

It is you that has given me the power to get wealth –Deut. 8:18

Surely goodness and mercy shall follow me- Psalm 23

You make my way prosperous and give me good success.

The Lord is my shepherd, I shall not want- Psalm 23

You maketh me to ly down in green pastures Psalm 23

I stand in agreement with the word of God over my life and call it done in the name of Yahshua Ha mashiach. I forbid any regrouping, reinforcement, surveillance and new strategies to have, hold or steal my possession and inheritance. Additionally, I put all legions, imps, and spirits on notice now that your time and works over my marriage, ministry, money, message, methods, maturity, morality, and motives must cease and desist now. I seal this prayer in the Holy Ghost and with the blood of Christ Jesus.

I declare Victory, Victory, Victory, Victory.

Holy Regards,

Name

Prayer For God Given Mate

*To be prayed at least 2x per day

Father, in the name of Jesus Christ I choose to worship you with my whole spirit, soul and body. I declare my undying love for you. For you are greater than Great. You are my everything Lord. In you I live, move and have my being. I set my love, passion and affection solely upon you, your purpose and assignment for my life. It is my heart's desire to serve you in every area of my life. For I desire you to lead me in the paths of righteousness for your name's sake. Father, I repent of all unholy and ungodly relationships, from fornication, sexual promiscuity, unfaithfulness and for whoring after other gods. Lord you are faithful and just to forgive me from all unrighteousness (1 John 1:9). Now Lord every power that is opposing and resisting my life partner from locating me be destroyed by fire in Jesus name. The filthy garments of singlehood that's driving away my mate catch a fire now in Jesus name. According to Isaiah 34:16, I declare my life partner is locating me now and increaseth in favour. For he that findeth a wife findeth a good thing and obtaineth favour of the Lord.

Your word says in all my ways I am to acknowledge you and you shall direct my path (Prov. 3:5). Order my steps, my heartbeat and love according to your word (Psalm 119:133). Matthew 7:7 says "Ask, and it shall be given me; seek and I shall find; knock and the door shall be opened unto me". I humbly ask for your perfect will to be done in my life and that I marry the man that was predestined for me before the foundation of the world and before I was formed in my mother's womb (Jer.1). You, Father, are the perfect matchmaker. Just as Eleazer was sent by Abraham to select an equally yoked bride for Isaac, I pray today that the Holy Spirit in like manner will locate and release the man, priest, king and prophet destined to reign alongside _____(your name). I declare and decree that every satanic barrier, border and quarantine established in the realm of the Spirit to hinder my marriage from taking place be dissolved and broken now in Jesus' name. I stand in the gap for my husband to be and loose him now from every ungodly soul tie, generational bondage, demonic addiction, physical limitations, curses, spells, omens, witchcraft/voodoo, mind manipulations and parental strings be destroyed by FIRE now in Jesus' name. I now call his soul, body and spirit out of darkness and into the marvelous light of Jesus Christ. Loose now Lord, Micheal and warfaring angels to wage warfare on his behalf. I reject every counterfeit spouse, distracting demonic spouse, fake spouse in Jesus name. I declare myself and husband to be loosed and free from any and all spirit wife/husband now in Jesus name. Every ungodly demonic blood covenant and satanic soul tie now be severed in the matchless name of Jesus Christ.

I bind and rebuke, forbid, disallow and disarm every:
- Player Spirit
- Jealous Spirit
- Scrub Spirit
- Leech Spirit
- Trickery Spirit
- Dog Spirit
- Obsessive Compulsive Spirit
- Lazy Spirit
- Homosexual Spirit
- Procrastination Spirit
- Ahab Spirit
- Carnal Spirit
- Vanity Spirit
- Abusive Spirit
- Mommy's Boy Spirit
- Nasty/Perverse Spirit
- Negligent Spirit

Father, I thank you for a mate like Abraham in Genesis 18:19 that will command his children and household after you Lord. A man of justice and good judgement that I can whole heartedly call Lord.

Lord I pray for a man with unwavering integrity like Joseph who has eyes, passion and love only for
_____ (your name). Thank you for a man with a faithful and loyal spirit like Joseph who will reign not only in the court of the Lord but also in the market place and have an anointing/gifts for business and rulership. A man that knows how to balance work and family life.

Lord, I thank you for a man like Jacob who will work and labour years if necessary to prove his authentic love for me and our family. A man like Jacob that would lose sleep wrestling/toiling all through the night until he gets a breakthrough for his lineage (generation). A man with a winner's anointing.

Lord, I bless you in advance for a king and prophet like David who would risk his life to ensure my safety and security. A man skilled in the art of spiritual warfare. One that would slay bears and Goliaths that we may walk in our Canaan Blessing.

Thank you Father for a priest like Elkanah, who will love me and respect me with all my flaws and inadequacies (1 Sam 1).

Lord, I bless you today for a King like Xerxes, who will go against his most trusted advisors/confidantes to stand by my side and grant me even to half of His kingdom.

A husband like Job who will have faith in you and trust you against all odds. Who will daily make intercession for his family and constantly present us before the throne of grace. A righteous man with impeccable moral and spiritual standards.

A king like Solomon who will publicly and passionately love me and satisfy all my heart and soul's desires in bed. A man that meets my needs emotionally (financially, relationally, etc); one whose love many waters cannot quench, neither will floods be able to drown and who will give all the substance of his house for my love (Song Of Solomon 8).

Thank you for a man that will redeem me from all past shame, hurt, disgrace and failure and be ecstatic to wed, provide and impregnate me like Boaz did with Ruth.

A husband and co-laborer In ministry like Aquila (Acts 18:2) who will be unashamed to proclaim the gospel of Christ Jesus and expand his kingdom on earth.

A man like Joseph who was assigned to Mary to facilitate the birthing of my God given assignment/ministry despite public opinion, rejection and marginalization.

Last, but definitely not least, thank you for a man like Christ Jesus that would give his very life for me and love me as his own flesh. A man that exemplifies the love, character and spirit of Jesus. One who will be with me to the very end.

A man who makes submission to his love easy.

This day I shall eat the fruit of my lips and I shall possess/have what I say. As I have spoken, let it be done unto me according to your perfect will. In the omnipotent name of Jesus Christ I pray, Amen. Amen & again I say, Amen.

Bibliography

Anderson, Neil. Winning Spiritual Warfare. (1990). Eugene, Oregon. Harvest House Publishers

Chavda, Mahesh. The Hidden Power of Prayer and Fasting. (1998). Shippensburg, PA. Whitaker House

Cho, David. Prayer That Brings Revival. (1998). Lake Mary, FL. Charisma House

Eckhardt, John. The Ministry Anointing Of The Prophet. (1995). Chicago, IL. Crusader Ministries.

Ing, Richard. Spirtual Warfare. (1996). New Kensington, PA. Whitaker House.

Murray, Andrew. The Ministry of Intercession. (1982). Springdale, PA. Whitaker House.

Towns, Elmer. Fasting For Spiritual Break Through. (1996). Ventura, CA. Regal Books

Trimm, Cindy. Prophets And Prophecy. (2011). Stockbridge, GA. Kingdom Life Publishing Company.

About The Author

"The Spirit of the Lord God is upon me; because the Lord hath anointed me to preach good tidings unto the meek; he hath sent me to bind up the broken-hearted, to proclaim liberty to the captives, and the opening of the prison to them that are bound; to proclaim the acceptable year of the Lord..." Isaiah 61:1-2

The Lord preordains and predestinates His leaders in every generation before birth. Jasmin Dareus has been groomed and graced with heaven's approval as a Voice Piece for this time and to this generation. The hand of the Lord has been evident on Jasmin's life from a very early age. Always the chosen leader, speaker and representative for her people. Given to the body of Christ in the office of the Prophet, Jasmin Dareus is fearlessly armed, radically anointed and heavily mantled with a relevant Prophetic & Miracle Grace with the living word of the Lord sharply in her mouth. Her feet has been steadily charged and shod with the gospel of peace. She is a woman of integrity, standard, honour, and love.

Jasmin Dareus hails from the quaint settlement of Fresh Creek, Central Andros, The Bahamas where she received her primary and secondary education. In 2003, she obtained her associate's degree in Biology from The College of the Bahamas. In 2004 she attended Barry University and majored in International Studies. Prophetically trained under Christian International founded by Dr. Bill Hammon (2008) and a graduate of Kingdom University whose Chancellor is Dr. Cindy Trimm (2014).

Jasmin A. P. Dareus is an international Speaker, Author, Educator, Leadership Mentor, and a Savvy Business Woman. Jasmin Dareus is the Co-Founder and Co Pastor of Kingdom Harvest Global Ministries which is a multicultural and a multidimensional organization head quartered in Freeport, Grand Bahama, Bahamas. Pastor Dareus is the President of K. H. G. Ministries School of the Prophet and "Daughter Arise" Women's Ministry. She is the Founder and Executive Producer of "Kingdom Living" television programme aired nationally in the Bahamas. Jasmin Dareus is married to Apostle Brian Dareus and both travel as itinerant speakers. Together, they have five gifted girls and many spiritual children.

Above all, Jasmin Dareus is the handmaiden of the Lord.

Ministry Resources

Books

Prevailing Prayer	$20.00
The Prophetic Mantle	$25.00
The Dream Realm	$20.00

DVD's

The Master Key Of Prayer (1)	$15.00
The Master Key Of Prayer (2)	$15.00
Favour	$15.00
Atonement Blessings	$15.00
The Nicolaitan Spirit	$15.00

CD's

Prayer of Healing	$10.00
Prophetic Declarations	$10.00
Warfare Prayer	$10.00

**Please add $4.00 for shipping and handling.

Contact Information

Prophetess Jasmin Dareus Ministries
P. O. Box F-44252
Freeport,
Grand Bahama,
Bahamas.

Email: jasmindareusministry@gmail.com

Telephone Contact:
1-242-439-0210 (Cell)
1-242-352-4241 (Church)

Made in the USA
Columbia, SC
24 December 2023